GREG FREEMAN

a
gentleman,
a gentle
man

Selected Columns, *St. Louis Post-Dispatch*

Foreword by Lorraine Kee

Introduction by Bill McClellan

Greg Freeman, A Gentleman, A Gentle Man

ISBN: 1-891442-23-6
Library of Congress Control Number: 2003106229
Published for the *St. Louis Post-Dispatch* by:
Virginia Publishing Corp.
P.O. Box 4538
St. Louis, MO 63108
(314) 367-6612

Table of Contents

Part 6: Wit and Wisdom   163

About The Author   190

Foreword
By Lorraine Kee

It was easy to be Greg's friend.

How could you not love a guy who was 46 but still got a trim when his mother told him his short-cropped hair was getting too long.

A guy who called his wife, Elizabeth, his "best friend."

Who never gave his son grief about his dreadlocks or whether he could support himself as an artist.

Who was sure enough of his masculinity that he could acknowledge that he didn't know the difference between the score and shots-on-goal at a hockey game or could only offer me sympathy — not a hammer or a hand — when my Christmas tree kept falling down the first holiday after my divorce.

A guy who loved office gossip, but never had a bad word to say about anyone. Who was nice to people even when they were rude to him.

Who loved working for a newspaper.

Who always saw potential in downtown St. Louis.

A guy who loved cats.

Who was the soul of the Greater St. Louis Association of Black Journalists.

Who liked to start meetings on time.

Who gave much and took little.

Who never complained when I saw him in the hospital through his prostate cancer, incarcerated hernia, his kidney transplant, his muscular dystrophy.

Who had a crooked smile.

Who loved his Beaumont High School reunions.

Who preached diversity in his columns and lived it in his life.

Who had cassette tapes in his car that ran the gamut from Motown to Smashing Pumpkins.

Who was equally comfortable eating sushi or snoots.

Who got way excited one day when we saw the gorgeous Pam Grier in a Washington restaurant.

Who made no apologies for loving those "Brady Bunch" movies.

Who warned me not to try to be hip in my columns because when middle-aged folks like us tried it we just sounded goofy.

Who I could tell everything to.

Who I knew would never hurt me.

Never insult me.

Never judge me.

Never laugh at me but with me.

Who knew everything there was to know about me and stayed my friend.

Who was such a loving friend that I could love him back.

Who imagined us old and gray someday.

Who I called four times on the Monday before he died.

Who didn't say a word when I lingered long at his house last Thanksgiving dinner, savoring the turkey and sopping up the warmth of his family.

A guy who could sing.

Years ago, when I got the wild inclination to sing at the

office Christmas party, even though I couldn't sing, I promptly asked Greg if he would sing with me. He had done it before and our colleagues loved him.

I can't sing by myself, I said. Would you? Could you?

He didn't hesitate. That was Greg. Supportive. We practiced. I bought huge Afro wigs. We sang. And I was awful. Of course, he never said that. He was too kind. He just didn't have mean in him.

The last two weeks we had both been racking our brains, trying to remember what song it was that we had performed that night at Blueberry Hill. Neither of us could remember, and we laughed that the memory was the first to go as you age. I'd remember one of these days, I told him. It would probably come to me in the middle of the night, I said, and I'd sit bolt upright in my bed. I'd let him know when I thought of it.

On Tuesday morning, I took the long walkway up to Greg and Elizabeth's place in the Central West End, and I felt an overwhelming sadness.

"Second That Emotion" popped into my head. That had been the song.

Jan. 5, 2003

Introduction
By Bill McClellan

The desk next to me is empty now, but the photographs are still in place. The most prominent is that of a thoughtful young man. His name is Will Freeman, and in the photo, he is wearing a bemused expression and dreadlocks.

He grew those dreadlocks during his first year at college, and when he returned home in the summer of 2000, his father wasn't quite sure what to make of the new hairstyle.

So the father wrote about his son's hair. Rather, he wrote about his own reaction.

"So far, I've remained pretty calm about it, which is less than my mother did when I was in college and grew a big Afro. I look back now at some of the pictures of myself during that time and laugh. Maybe a time will come when Will will do the same. Meanwhile, I'll just have to grin and bear it."

He ended that column this way: "The future is in the hands of people like my son. I must say that those are pretty good hands."

That was, as readers of this newspaper know, quintessential Greg Freeman. Always keeping things in perspective, always ending on a hopeful note. To Greg, the world was a pretty nice place.

It is a little less so right now for the rest of us. Greg died Tuesday.

He was a most unusual person. I sat next to him, and chatted with him on a regular basis, and I never heard him say a mean word about anybody. I mean that literally. Never a mean word. That would be remarkable for a person with a normal job, but for a newspaper columnist, it's unbelievable. In our business, it is understood that a story flies better if it has a villain for a wing, and most of us are guilty, at one time or another, of trying to squeeze somebody into the villain's suit even if the fit isn't quite right. But not Greg. He went the other way. He always gave people the benefit of the doubt.

What an honorable way to do this job.

But that was Greg. Honorable, gentlemanly and without pretension. That, too, is most unusual for a newspaper columnist. Most of us like to affect an air of detachment. It seems, somehow, intellectual.

Not Greg. I remember a couple of years ago when he wrote about his 25th high school reunion. He wrote that his wife, Elizabeth, didn't go to her high school reunions, and had, in fact, put high school behind her, while he not only went to his Beaumont High School reunions, he helped plan them. He was, after all, the former senior class president.

It was easy to see, even years later, why the class had elected him.

Readers of this newspaper have known for a while that Greg has had health problems. In the fall of 2000, he was hit with two awful bits of news. First, he was told that he had a form of muscular dystrophy. Less than a month later, he was told that his kidneys were failing. He eventually wrote about both of those things, and we readers were even allowed into the operating room with him 13 months ago when he received a kidney from his sister, Cheryl McKinney.

Here's a strange thing, though. He wrote about those things, and he did so almost reverently, but he did not talk about them. He did not complain.

Exactly two weeks before Christmas, he spoke at a fundraiser for the St. Louis Society. He was, by then, confined to a wheelchair. He sat in front of the audience, and he talked about how he had tried to hide his disability from his friends. He put off using a cane for as long as possible. He even resisted the idea of a special license plate. But things worked out, he said. By the time he could no longer hide the fact that his muscles were failing, he had concluded that he was not going to be hindered by this so-called disability, anyway. He could still host a radio show on KWMU. He could still write his newspaper column.

Those columns will be missed. They reflected their author. Kind and cheerful and always hopeful. But not in a naive way. Greg had a deep appreciation for the fragility of life. His father, Frederic Freeman, was a postal clerk who was killed in an accident at work when Greg was 14.

Last year, a friend's father died, and Greg wrote about what it's like to lose your father.

"I suppose that if there was never any love between my father and me, his death wouldn't have been very painful. He would have simply been a person who had left my life. But because there was so much love, the pain has been greater. In my case, and in the case of my friend, the pain probably never goes away. But neither, fortunately, does the love."

That's a message of hope for the young man whose photograph sits on the desk next to mine. The love never goes away.

Jan 1, 2003

Part 1:

City
Life

HOW TO REVIVE DOWNTOWN?
START WITH TUNES, FOOD

Imagine a Downtown St. Louis filled with marvelous sights, sounds and smells.

Street vendors sell a dozen types of smoked wurst. Two young men with drumsticks play upside-down, white plastic buckets to the delight of an appreciative crowd. A man sitting nearby plays old blues tunes on a bass guitar.

Nearby, a bearded man who looks to be in his early 40s is dressed up in an Uncle Sam outfit, selling handmade puppets. Around the corner, two young men display their juggling talents with bowling pins as a small group circles and applauds.

This isn't the downtown St. Louis we now know. But it's one we could know if our elected officials would consider changing a few ordinances.

Mayor Clarence Harmon and the Board of Aldermen are getting all sorts of free advice this week. Charles Brennan of KMOX radio and I want to add a bit more: Help bring color and life to downtown by allowing street musicians and vendors. Downtown would be well served by their addition.

Brennan and I are on a mission to bring them to the streets of downtown. (And it would be nice to have them in other areas as well, including Soulard and the Central West End.)

I was on Brennan's "Morning Meeting" program earlier this week, and he and I — along with John Ferrara of Pasta House Co. fame — agreed that the musicians and vendors would give downtown a much-needed flavor.

Right now, vendors and street musicians are prohibited downtown. Several years ago, the Board of Aldermen approved legislation banning them from the area. Some thought the problem of panhandling and aggressive vending was getting out of hand. The result was a ban on street sales and street musicians in most of downtown.

No one wants to be grabbed by a vendor who insists on selling something. But it would be easy enough to license vendors to make sure they're regulated.

Downtown needs life. While it has its pockets of night life — a few restaurants near Market Street, the Laclede's Landing area — much of it is dead at night, and the number of dead areas during the day is growing.

Street vendors and musicians can't change all of that. But they can give people a reason to be downtown. You can eat at a restaurant in a pristine suburban mall, or you can dine outdoors downtown while strolling musicians go by. While it's doubtful that people would come downtown solely for street vendors or musicians, they would add to the ambience of downtown and make it more attractive for people to visit.

There has been so much wringing of hands — and rightly so — in the past few months about the city's deteriorating downtown. A key problem, pointed out by various experts, is that very few live there. Why not? One reason may be that downtown is not nearly as interesting as it could be. Musicians and vendors would help make it a more interesting place.

What visitor can go to New York without trying one of those New York hot dogs sold on the street, the messy kind with mustard and sauerkraut? Is there any good reason why tourists and locals alike wouldn't care to munch on original St. Louis hot dogs?

Sometimes we're so staid here, so afraid of change. But the kind of change that Brennan and I are proposing isn't revolutionary. Plenty of cities see the value in vendors and musicians. New York, Cambridge, Mass., and Chicago, to name but three. If our own city is to get out of the rut we're in, we've got to be willing to think unconventionally, to be willing to stop doing things a certain way simply because we've always done them that way.

Surely any effort to revive downtown should include allowing musicians and vendors to hit the streets. It makes no sense to ban a potential people magnet from downtown.

Some suggest that downtown is withering on the vine. That description is a bit too harsh, but it's clear that downtown could be so much more. Vendors and musicians may seem to be only a small part of what downtown needs to blossom, but Brennan and I contend that it's an important part.

Perhaps the mayor or a progressive-thinking alderman will take this issue on and try to change the ordinances that have kept downtown from being as lively as it could be. Changing the ordinances would be a real boon, not just for downtown, but for the area. *(April 17, 1997)*

STREET ENTERTAINERS NEED MORE THAN JUST WARM APPLAUSE

You get what you pay for.

Three years ago, KMOX radio's Charles Brennan and I started a campaign.

In an effort to make the streets of downtown livelier, Brennan and I encouraged lawmakers to change ordinances to allow street vendors and entertainers on the streets of downtown. Both had been banned years before, in an effort to make downtown's streets more pristine.

Brennan and I argued that vendors and street performers would enliven the place. Much of downtown was dead, we argued, and these efforts would awaken the place and give it some color.

The public responded and so did the lawmakers. A bill was introduced, and the Board of Aldermen passed it.

The result? Today, vendors are seen on various streets downtown, selling soda, hot dogs, bratwurst and other culinary treats. And whenever I've passed by them, they've always been busy with customers. In fact, St. Louisans have voted for the vendors with their feet.

But what we've seen very little of are street entertainers. I had envisioned guitarists singing on the streets of downtown, young men with drumsticks playing upside-down white plastic buckets to the delight of an appreciative crowd, mimes performing for a giddy audience.

But the streets of downtown are virtually void of entertainers, although the city has issued 22 permits for busking, or street entertaining.

Why?

The answer seems to be that we St. Louisans are cheap.

One man who tried his hand at street entertaining downtown explained it to me this way: "I'd play my guitar and sing folk tunes," he said. "People really seemed to love them. They'd gather around and clap, and sometimes they'd even sing along to a song. But when it came time to put something in the guitar case — well, I guess most people thought that applause was enough."

We are, of course, frugal Midwesterners. Unlike places like New York, where the rich often flaunt their wealth and spend money freely, our wealthy, like the rest of us, tend to be conservative when it comes to money. Why pay for music when you can hear it for free?

Our great desire to get something for nothing isn't just with street entertainers, of course.

The Bi-State Development Agency, which for years operated MetroLink on the honor system, now requires you to have a ticket to be on the platform. Apparently, more than a few riders had chosen the free route.

Still, when it comes to street entertainers, our cheapness is robbing us of good entertainment downtown. OK, I'll concede that not everyone likes a mime. But street musicians, singers, even break dancers can be fun to watch. And just as few of us work for free, neither do they.

Lots of effort is being spent these days to make downtown special again. But downtowns aren't special just because they've got a stadium or glistening new buildings. Downtowns are special when they're fun places to go, places people want to be, where they want to linger.

Street vendors are part of that. So are street entertainers. While no one's going to head downtown just to see street entertainers, they add to the ambience and help make it a place where people want to be.

The politicians did their part. They passed laws that let it happen.

Now it's up to us to do our parts.

Come on, St. Louisans. The next time you see a street entertainer downtown, whether it's someone singing or a person doing magic tricks, toss him a quarter. Better yet, toss him a dollar.

It's not only good for the entertainer, it's good for the city. *(June 29, 2000)*

FED UP WITH TORN-UP STREET, BUSINESS OWNER HEADS FOR THE SUBURBS

After nearly 50 years in the same location, the little store at 1317 Washington Avenue will close its doors on Monday.

Anatol's Fabric Outlet, the city's only fabric outlet store, is calling it quits — at least as far as downtown is concerned. The store is moving to Webster Groves.

Fed up with months of street closings and construction work being done on Washington that have harmed his business, owner Robert Tamsky has had enough. Tamsky says he wasn't dying to go. "I hate to leave downtown," Tamsky said. "I guess I'll be questioning my decision to leave for the rest of my life. But all the other fabric stores that were once downtown left 30 years ago."

Tamsky said he had considered staying downtown. "But we needed more space, and I couldn't get a lease anywhere around here that would extend past the date when the construction is due to be finished," he said.

A peek through Anatol's window reveals cramped quarters filled with yards and yards of fabric — a tailor's dream. The store — in the heart of downtown's old garment district — was founded by Tamsky's grandfather, Anatol Tamsky, in 1952.

"Our retail, walk-in business is less than half it was before the construction started," Robert Tamsky said. "Fortunately for us, we have a decent wholesale and Internet sales business." (The Web address is www.bridalfabric.com.)

The torn-up streets and street closings are part of a renovation effort for Washington Avenue. The plan is to beautify the street and widen the sidewalks. The city promises that it will mean a bright future for businesses there, but many of those enduring the construction are frustrated by how long the work is taking.

Tamsky isn't the only business owner to complain about the work, which has also made parking on the street harder to find. "They did the water lines three or four times, then the gas lines, then the cable lines — and I don't even know if it's going to work or not," Tamsky said.

"A lot of companies are losing business during this street debacle, and I suspect ours won't be the only one to leave," he said.

Tamsky said that when he was trying to figure out a way to remain downtown, he reached out to "Downtown St. Louis, Downtown Now, one of those downtown groups," but didn't receive much help. Instead, he said, he got a flier in the mail urging him to join and an invitation to attend a $45 lunch.

"Their interest seemed to be to simply get me to pay dues and join their organization," he said. "So I didn't take it any further."

Anatol's is best known for its sale of wedding fabric — wedding gowns, bridesmaids' dresses, veils, gloves and the like. One of the company's specialties is outfitting African-American weddings. Customers often go to Anatol's looking for fabric and a dressmaker. Typically a bride will bring photos from bridal magazines to show what style she wants.

Anatol's also sells fabric for dancers and skaters, and in recent years has added home decorator fabrics.

Tamsky is not sure when he will open his new store, at 235 East Kirkham Avenue in Webster Groves. "As soon as I get unpacked, we'll open," he said. Meanwhile, his Internet site will continue to operate without interruption.

The loss of a business like Anatol's isn't major news like the loss of a major downtown corporation. But the small businesses are the ones that keep downtown going. They deserve more attention than the city and downtown business groups often give them. When they're ignored, many of them do what Anatol's is doing — they pick up and leave. As efforts continue to get new people and businesses downtown, the powers that be shouldn't forget those who are already there, those who have gone through good times and bad.

As for Tamsky, he says he will miss working downtown. "We've been here a long time," he said. "But it's time to move on." *(July 29, 2001)*

WEEDING OUT SOME ORDINANCES COULD MAKE ST. LOUIS MORE USER-FRIENDLY

Bart Simpson, stay out of downtown St. Louis, if you know what's good for you.

If you're not careful, you could wind up just like 14-year-old Baron Mitchell.

Baron might appear to be a fine, upstanding lad. He's an honor student. Gets straight A's. But that didn't prevent him from being stopped by one of St. Louis's finest last week. His crime? Skateboarding.

Baron had been in an office with his dad, Bob Mitchell, who works at a building downtown. Around lunchtime, Baron decided to head to a fast-food restaurant to grab something to eat.

He strapped his helmet on, jumped on his skateboard and was promptly stopped by an officer. He was told that it's illegal to skateboard on the streets or sidewalks of downtown.

The officer gave Baron a warning, who was surprised by the whole thing.

"My mom is in Huntsville, and I've always skated there without any problem," he said. "I've skated here a couple of times and never been told that it was against the law."

Bob Mitchell was surprised by the whole thing as well.

"He's a good kid, and he doesn't cause trouble," Mitchell said. "The whole thing doesn't make much sense to me."

Even some police officers shake their heads.

"It's the law, so we've got to enforce it," one officer said. "I can think of better laws than this one, though."

So can Heath Finn. Finn is upset because his wife got a parking ticket on the street where he lives in the city's West End. Her ticket was for parking within 10 feet of a mailbox.

"Fifteen dollars," Heath Finn said. "Ouch!"

Finn says he doesn't mind paying parking tickets.

"I've gotten a few tickets over the years because my parking meter ran out, and I don't mind paying those," he said. "But 10 feet from a mailbox? I never even heard of that.

"I could understand it better if most houses in the city had driveways and garages. But when you have to park on the street, it doesn't seem right that you should have to get a ticket."

Finn moved to the city six years ago from rural Illinois. After moving here, he got married. His wife is from St. Charles.

"With no small effort, I convinced her to live in the city," he said. "I am an advocate of the city and its revitalization efforts and, in general, I am pleased with living here. I enjoy the atmosphere, central location, diversity and the convenience of walking to do most of my errands.

"I'm well aware of the city's financial problems, but nickel-and-diming employed, productive citizens is not the answer."

Finn says that for most people, it's not worth it to take the time off to go to court to contest a parking ticket.

"So we just pay the ticket, even if we don't think it's right," he said. "Still, it seems the city could build some good will if it wouldn't be so quick to issue parking tickets."

Yes, Baron and Finn were breaking the law. So are the people who park at one-hour meters and go to a ball game, only to find tickets on their windshields when they return.

Skateboarding downtown, parking within 10 feet of a mailbox, not putting more money into a meter during a ball game

— all are against the law, and the city is within its rights to ticket people for these things. Still, it seems that government at times can have too many laws on its books. In the eyes of many, St. Louis is close to being one of those governments.

In a city that continues to bleed population, it might make sense for lawmakers to look at the ordinances on the books to see how to make them more people-friendly. More laws don't necessarily make a city better. When residents believe the parking ticket system is unjust — or suggest that the only efficient operation the city has going is the ticket-writing process — what message are you sending to taxpayers?

Maybe I'm just looking for a kinder, gentler city government.

But considering the problems St. Louis faces and the work it's putting into getting people to live in the city (and fewer people from moving out) it seems that such efforts would be in order.

It wouldn't hurt St. Louis to lighten up a bit. *(May 28, 2000)*

SNUB STEAMS URBAN DWELLER

Gloria Ross was still steaming when I returned her call.

"I'm really upset about this," she said. "It's as if I'm being redlined."

The object of Ross's ire was not an insurance company, though. Instead, it was Stanley Steemer Carpet Cleaner.

Ross, who needed her carpets and sofa cleaned, had seen a commercial for the company and had called to find out more about it.

"The woman who answered the phone told me all about the excellent quality of the company's services and how they took pride and care in their work," she said. "I asked them if my not living on the first floor was a problem and she even assured me that it wasn't, that the company went everywhere necessary to do a good job."

Everywhere, it turned out, but Ross's ZIP code.

"I decided I wanted them to come clean, and she asked my ZIP code," Ross said. "When I told her I lived in 63112, she told me that the company didn't serve areas in the city of St. Louis. I wasn't in the company's service area. And when I asked who served my area, she said no one.

"I was astounded. There are some very nice homes here."

Ross, who lives in the DeBaliviere Place area, bristled when she was told that the company — which only minutes before had been described to her by the saleswoman as very accommodating — would not come to her home.

When Ross asked questions, the saleswoman let her speak with the manager. He explained to her that service areas are based on average incomes. Apparently the average income of her ZIP code wasn't high enough to attract the cleaning company.

I took a look at a ZIP code map and saw that the 63112 area code is a broad one. It stretches from an area just north of Dr. Martin Luther King Boulevard to Forest Park Parkway on the south. It stretches between Union Avenue on the east and Skinker Boulevard on the west. It includes both tony mansions on Lindell Boulevard and run-down housing near the city limits that border on Wellston.

"At first I was shocked," Ross said. "Then I was in utter disbelief. And then I was angry.

"What difference does it make how much money the ZIP code makes? I'm the one paying for the work, not the ZIP code . . . They suggested that I call Famous-Barr or Sears."

I placed several calls to the manager with whom she had spoken but never heard back from him.

Ross said the incident bothered her.

"It's just another indignity that we suffer for living in the city," she said. "I sometimes feel that I'm being penalized for living in the city."

And for Ross, a working professional who says she'd live nowhere else, it's frustrating.

Carpet cleaning isn't the only problem, says Ross, who once lived in St. Louis County. "I have to pay more for car insurance and for renter's insurance. It doesn't seem to matter whether there's crime in the area where you live or not, whether you park on a lot with an automated gate or not. It's the fact that I live in the city."

And it's not just cleaning services or insurance. Depending on where you live, it can be tough to get certain types of pizza delivered. Rarely will you get one of those companies that delivers food from selected restaurants to come into the city.

"There are people who live in the county who won't come to visit because they think it's not safe," she said. "People think I'm a fool for living here. They think the whole city is dangerous, that they're going to be killed or something. It's not that way at all.

"I know people who ask me, 'How do you go home at night?' Isn't that ridiculous?"

As most city residents know, the entire city is not dangerous. Your chances in many neighborhoods of being murdered are about as great as your chances of being in a fatal traffic accident. Without a doubt, some areas exist in which you shouldn't walk the streets at night. Of course, St. Louis County, Madison and St. Clair counties have similar areas. Common sense would tell you to stay out of those places.

But to stereotype city neighborhoods — as some companies and individuals do — is without a doubt unfair to the hard-working, law-abiding residents of St. Louis. The city isn't as crime-ridden as some would think.

For many, St. Louis is a good place to live. It would be a better place without the stereotypes. *(Oct. 29, 1993)*

LOOK AT OTHER CITIES, AND YOU MIGHT STOP GRIPING ABOUT OURS

"Dear Greg: How can you stand St. Louis? The city's shot to hell, the people are snobs and the area has very little redeeming value. We'll never be a city like Chicago . . ."

That was the way one reader started his letter to me. I get comments like these every so often from St. Louisans who are fed up with this place.

While I appreciate the letter-writer's point of view, I don't agree with him. His letter is a reflection of the inferiority complex that many St. Louisans share.

I love St. Louis. It's not perfect, but what city is?

Sure, we've got our share of problems. But are they really that much worse than any other urban area?

Let's re-examine some typical complaints from St. Louisans.

* Traffic here is atrocious. Rush hour traffic on Interstate 70 at the Blanchette Bridge is unbearable. Interstate 64 at 270 is a killer.

Yeah, right.

You could always live in Silicon Valley, home of the nation's computer whizzes. It's gorgeous and it's pristine. But the traffic? The freeways are more like parking lots during rush hour or, more accurately, rush hours. Getting caught in traffic in San Jose, Calif., will make you beg for an old-fashioned St. Louis traffic jam.

* The people in St. Louis aren't friendly.

Which people are you talking to? Folks from this area, in general, are inherently friendly. Don't believe it? Next time you're on the highway, turn on your left turn signal to change to the next lane. Chances are, a car in the next lane will happily let you pass. Now try that in Chicago. Your left turn light will probably burn out before someone lets you pass. If you're lucky, the car in the next lane won't speed up.

* It's too hot in the summertime.

I was born here and have never gotten used to St. Louis summers. But is there really a perfect city for weather? Seattle sounds great, but it rains frequently. Minneapolis is great in the summer, but it easily makes up for it with its below-zero winter temperatures. New York is a great place, but it gets as hot as St. Louis in the summertime. There's no perfect city for weather in the United States.

* The schools are lousy.

In fact, St. Louis schools aren't much different than most public schools in urban areas. Many public schools these days face serious challenges — but a person moving from one urban school district to another is likely to find the same problems, if not worse, elsewhere.

* It's getting too expensive to buy a house here.

Home prices aren't going down anywhere, but you can probably get a better bargain in St. Louis than anywhere else. A perusal of a recent Los Angeles Times showed a home there with three bedrooms and two baths going for $565,000. Want to look the other way? How about a two-bedroom home in a not-so-great neighborhood in Queens, N.Y.? A mere $295,000, according to an ad in the New York Daily News. Homes may not be as inexpensive in St. Louis as they once were, but it takes leaving this place to appreciate the prices here.

The old saying about the grass being greener somewhere else certainly makes sense when the talk turns to cities. We often don't appreciate what we have — at least not until others notice it.

A Philadelphian visiting St. Louis once remarked to me how clean downtown St. Louis is. I hadn't really noticed until he made those comments. After that, I paid closer attention to many of the other downtowns that I visited, and I realized that he was right.

I've visited many cities over the years. Through it all, I've come away with one general impression: This is a pretty good place. *(July 17, 2001)*

A TALE ABOUT HOW ST. LOUIS BECAME THE HOT PLACE TO BE

'Twas the night before Christmas
and all through the city
the trees were all up.
The lights were so pretty.
Mayor Harmon was nestled
all snug in his bed
while a sparkling new downtown
danced in his head.
Buzz Westfall was sleeping
free from tension
as he dreamed about the
Page Avenue extension.
And on the East Side
Mayor Gordon Bush slumbered
knowing his days
as mayor were numbered.
Roger Wilson wasn't able
to sleep through the night
because to make ends meet
he had to moonlight.

But members of St. Louis
2004
dreamed of ways to make
this region soar.
Elsewhere, William Danforth
dreamed of a neat
resolution to deseg. 'Twas
no easy feat.
When suddenly downtown
there arose such a clatter
this columnist awoke
to see what was the matter.
I hopped in my car
and drove toward the sound
speeding and weaving
toward downtown.
As I sped through the city
my car was stopped
by Chief Ron Henderson,
the city's top cop.
I told him of this matter
of great import
and he let me go
with a police escort.
We arrived at the Arch grounds
and were startled to see
a fat man with a beard —
and that man wasn't me!
His beard was white
and his suit was bright red.
"Not exactly fashionable,"
to Henderson I said.
Still, his eyes were bright

and his stomach like Jell-O.
He certainly seemed
like a good-natured fellow.
This stranger had arrived
on a large riverboat.
It wasn't the Admiral,
This boat could float
And move down the river.
It had come quite quickly.
He'd come by boat
for his reindeer were sickly.
But that didn't stop him
from going straight to his work.
He observed his surroundings,
then turned with a jerk.
He reached in the bag
filled with dusty old plans
that once had been written
by rich consultants.
He called out their names
and as I stood gazing
The plans came alive.
It was quite amazing.
"On, Kiel Opera House! Live once again!
On, Chase Hotel! It's time to open!
On, East Side Music Center! Become a star!
On, Arena site, whatever you are!"
"On, connection between downtown and Laclede's
Landing!
On, Federal Courthouse! Give St. Louis standing!
On, Grand Center! Be one of the city's bright lights!
On, St. Louis region! No more urban sprawl fights!"
He kept shouting out projects

Greg Freeman: A Gentleman, A Gentle Man

And calling their names.
They came to life at a speed
to put planners to shame.
"On, convention hotel! Arise from your slumber!
On, Six Flags water park! Folks will want you in summer!
On, loft district! Grow up and live long!
On, St. Charles! May your future be strong!"
And suddenly St. Louis came really alive
from the greatest location to the lowest dive.
The region became bright, we became a star,
The envy of cities both near and far.
The city and counties stopped fighting and
joined as a region. It was something quite grand.
Despite a past of much tension and strife,
we became a hot city. We had a nightlife!
In the day there was plenty for families to do.
Street performers abounded; hot-dog venders too.
People migrated here from across the nation.
St. Louis was, frankly, a national sensation.
Santa finished his job and looked around.
It was just what he wanted. A thriving downtown
and a prosperous region that thought outside the box.
To heck with Cleveland! St. Louis Rocks!
And as he packed up his bag to go,
Santa called out a jolly "Ho ho ho!"
He got back on his boat and he cruised out of sight
Saying, "Merry Christmas, St. Louis, and to you a good
night!" *(Dec. 24, 1998)*

IMAGINE METROLINK MURALS THAT TEACH HISTORY AS YOU RIDE

Writing the sort of column that I do, it's not unusual for

me to get letters from readers with ideas for the city.

Some of them have ideas that seem to hold merit. Other ideas are, well . . . Let's just call them difficult to imagine.

But a regular reader of my online forum, "Greg Freeman's Front Porch," made a suggestion recently that I thought held merit. She followed up on it with me in several e-mails.

The reader, who modestly asked me to refer to her only as Emma, thinks her project would be a good one for a collaboration between Mayor Francis Slay and new Bi-State chief Larry Salci.

Emma's idea is to use both MetroLink stops and the trains themselves to tell the city's history through murals. "Tourists would love it, and I think it would help connect more locals to our colorful past," she wrote.

"Our French/Spanish colonial past alone is so rich and entertaining, including women and blacks (free and slave) and Indians. But we're also the product of so many 19th and early 20th century immigration waves — Irish, German, Italian, Scottish, Swedish, Syrian/Lebanese, Russian, Czech, Hungarian, Chinese, etc. We even had a Chinatown located around, I believe, somewhere close to Busch Stadium."

Emma would put Slay in charge, "deferring to his wisdom and experience in actually getting things done." Slay would appoint a team ("let's not call it a commission or blue-ribbon panel, which would mean the project would be doomed from the start").

The team would develop a plan, work on themes for each stop and determine the characters and events to be included in the murals. The team would do this with input from the public, the result of hearings where professionals and amateurs alike would pass along their thoughts.

Once the themes, characters and events were established, the team would establish a competition for specific design ideas for each stop from local artists and wannabe artists. The mayor and team would choose the winning designs. A blind judging process would be set up so that lobbying wouldn't come into play.

"I figure the only real costs would be paint-and-brush-type expenses," Emma wrote. "Rather than pay for this project with corporate sponsors who would require free advertising in the form of having their logos plastered all over the murals, we'd come up with some kind of raffle where neighborhood organizations sold tickets, with half going to the organizations and half going to the Train Mural Fund. Perhaps tickets could also be sold at city offices.

"This is going to sound goofy to anybody who doesn't know St. Louisans' affections for gambling and feeling important by thinking they personally know elected officials, but I was thinking we could get the city and county office holders to coordinate raffle prizes like Honorary Mayor, Honorary Comptroller, Honorary License Collector, Honorary Assessor, Honorary Parks Commissioner, Honorary Fire Chief For A Day. Winners would get to hang out with the official official, a personal tour of their honorary empire, a certificate suitable for framing, lunch, and maybe attend some semi-important function.

"I know tons of people who would each fork over five bucks for five chances or whatever to become Honorary Whatever under this kind of scenario."

The raffle tickets also would let everyday people have a personal sense of ownership and acquire an excitement for the murals and even MetroLink.

"Can't you see it now?" Emma wrote. "Folks taking relatives on a MetroLink trip to see 'their' mural."

Sounds like an intriguing idea to me. Mr. Slay and Mr. Salci, are you listening? *(Feb. 12, 2002)*

LANDMARK SHOULD BE USED AS MUSEUM, FOR PERFORMANCES

If I didn't know better, I'd think someone had it in for Kiel Opera House.

You know the Opera House. It's the dignified building on Market Street guarded by two great bears on each side of its entrance. It's a St. Louis landmark that has been host to countless operas, rock groups, plays and even high school graduations.

When it was shuttered in 1991, it was with great anticipation. Kiel Center Partners had formed, with plans to replace the old Kiel Auditorium with Kiel Center, a brand-spanking new arena for major sports events and big concerts. The partners also promised to renovate the Opera House, cleaning it up and bringing the historic structure up to date.

As we all know, the center was built. Then, the partners decided it would cost too much money to renovate the Opera House.

After noise was made by fans of the building, the Urban Land Institute conducted a study that said St. Louis wouldn't support the Opera House along with other city cultural institutions, such as the Fox Theatre. Because the city's population has dwindled, that study concluded, the region could no longer support the Opera House.

Opera House supporters found that odd, given that the Opera House and the Fox had both existed until the Kiel Center Partners closed it. And the suggestion that it could no longer be supported because of a dwindling city population didn't seem to make a lot of sense, either. Census figures indicate that while the city may have lost population, the region has remained fairly static. People are moving around in this region, but they're neither coming nor going in droves. If the Opera House was affected by a smaller city population, what about the Cardinals? The Rams? Fair St. Louis? Are fewer people attending those events as well?

The Urban Land Institute's suggestion left plenty of people scratching their heads.

Now, St. Louis 2004 has issued a report saying that the arts are best left in other places like Grand Center. St. Louis should abandon Kiel Opera House as a performing arts site, it says. Those consultants want to energize Grand Center, and suggest that one way of doing that might be to build a 1,200- to 1,800-seat theater in that area.

That suggestion left me with more questions.

Why build a new theater if you have one downtown already? Do the consultants think that people will travel to Grand Boulevard but won't go downtown, only a mile or two east? And is there any reason why the Opera House can't be converted to support smaller arts groups, the jazz and blues hall of fame that Comptroller Darlene Green has suggested, and a Smithsonian satellite museum? And finally, isn't it possible to revitalize Grand Center without cannibalizing the Opera House entirely?

Just last week, consultants for Downtown Now spoke during a public forum about the lack of activity downtown between Union Station and Tucker Boulevard. Between them, pedestrians pass a post office, a federal building and the closed Opera House. Not exactly a barrel of laughs.

Put a hall of fame, a museum and a performance center in that same Opera House and you've managed to enliven an otherwise dull area. Ultimately, it adds much-needed color to downtown.

Clearly, people are all over the board on the Opera House, with some who would prefer that it never reopen as a performance site, and others, like longtime Kiel supporter Ed Golterman, who would love to see it restored to its original purpose.

It seems some sort of compromise ought to be possible, which would put this venerable institution back into service without completely abandoning its original mission.

What's needed here, more than anything else, is leadership and, ultimately, consensus. So far, no one's been able to provide that.

The Opera House is part of our heritage. It means a great deal to many St. Louisans, and it's an attractive, dignified old building that should be put to good use. Let's hope we're able to check our egos at the door and work on a viable solution that will save the Opera House and let it take its place once again as one of downtown's anchors. *(Dec. 15, 1998)*

METROPOLIS ADS SING ST. LOUIS' PRAISES WITHOUT BEATING OTHER CITIES DOWN

A year ago, when the Regional Chamber and Growth Association released a series of spots around the theme, "St. Louis — We got it good," the offbeat television commercials got lots of good reviews.

The chamber's ads — designed to air both in St. Louis and out of town — produced chuckles from viewers. The ads pointed out what St. Louis has over other cities. One that sticks with me most is the one that features a couple of apparent die-hard Boston fans who are complaining about how lousy Boston's teams are (this was obviously shot before this year's Super Bowl win by the New England Patriots). Another features a twentyish young man who's recently moved from St. Louis to New York, talking on the phone to his folks back home, telling them how roomy his new apartment is and what a great deal it is for only $1,900 a month, while the camera shows that his place is so tiny the bathroom is in the kitchen.

The spots were an attempt to shore up St. Louisans' self-esteem. One not-so-endearing trait of St. Louisans, noted previously in this column and elsewhere, is a willingness to put down our city, to regularly assume that every other large city is better than ours. The ads tried to point out that St. Louisans shouldn't have an inferiority complex, that we have countless advantages over other cities that we often take for granted.

But while some thought the ads were funny, some members of Metropolis St. Louis did not. "I didn't think that St. Louis had to put other cities down to make itself feel good," said Metropolis member Steve Smith. "There just seemed to be something unseemly about that whole thing."

Smith didn't just gripe; he did something about it. With financial help from Metropolis, Smith spent the last year, along with film director Marc Syp, developing a different ad campaign.

Among the differences has been the cost of putting the spots together. The RCGA spent several thousand dollars for their spots; the new 30-second ads developed by Metropolis were made for $2,000 - and lots of volunteer work.

One spot features a Saturday at Soulard Market. While an old blues tune plays in the background, the camera shows colorful produce being sold, a diverse crowd shopping, and people enjoying themselves as they inspect the market's goods. At the end of the spot, words subtly pop up on the screen that say, "Soulard Market." Then the words appear: "This is St. Louis." Smith says the completed ads will also feature the Metropolis Web site, www.mstl.org.

Among other spots are those that feature scenes of MetroLink as it travels across the Eads Bridge from Missouri to Illinois, as an upbeat tune plays in the background; a car of young people driving through all sorts of different neighborhoods in the city in a piece called "Exploring"; an especially arty spot featuring the World's Fair Pavilion at Forest Park during a thunderstorm; and a group of people being greeted by a priest after Mass at St. Alphonsus "Rock" Church. Another spot planned will feature a couple from Chicago who moved to a St. Louis neighborhood they feel is perfect.

Smith, who came up with the ideas for the spots, said he "didn't want to put together ads that said other cities suck."

"After all, if people want to live in Chicago or New York or somewhere else, ads criticizing those cities aren't likely to change their minds," Smith said. "We also didn't want to brag or say things like 'we're the best city in the world.' Instead, we wanted to point out what makes St. Louis unique, what makes this city stand out, what makes people from other cities choose St. Louis to live."

Smith has volunteered his time to get them produced. Syp, the film director, volunteered his time as well. Meanwhile, Barlow Studios donated their studios for the editing of the spots.

While the ads aren't quite ready to air yet — a couple more need to be shot — Smith says he and Metropolis will be approaching television stations here shortly, asking them to air the public service announcements.

The ads are sharp, and they would be terrific for St. Louisans — and non-St. Louisans as well — to see. They may help stem our city's inferiority complex.

After all, St. Louis has bucketloads of assets. The ads remind us of many of them. *(March 10, 2002)*

Part 2:

Family

THE MOST IMPORTANT MAN IN THE WORLD

It was only a small item in the *Post-Dispatch* that ran on June 1, 1971.

A man was killed in an accident at the Main Post Office.

Frederic W. Freeman, 44, a postal clerk, was crushed to death Sunday by a trailer on the parking lot of the Main Post Office, 1710 Clark Avenue.

Lamont Houston, 2424 Gaty Avenue, East St. Louis, backed a tractor to hook up a trailer, and Freeman, unseen by Houston, was crushed against a loading dock, police reported.

Frederic W. Freeman was my father. He was no big shot. His job wasn't a prominent one. He didn't rub shoulders with the wealthy or the powerful. But to our family, he was the most important man in the world.

We — my mother, my 10-year-old sister and I, 14 at the time — were devastated when we learned the news. Our world had changed. No longer would there be someone to tell me to "stop watching so much TV and let's go out and throw a ball." Gone was the man I would laugh at when he and my mother did "old-fashioned" dancing in the living room when they played a record on the hi-fi. No longer around was the man who made the best home-made biscuits this side of Pillsbury.

Not a week goes by now that I don't think about my dad.

I compare myself to him often, sometimes observing my own skills as a parent and wondering how they measure up to his, other times wondering how he would respond in certain situations.

The advice he offered when he was alive I remember today like the 10 Commandments; advice such as, "Nothing good comes easy," and "If you're going to do something, do it right or don't do it at all."

Not quite proverbs, but words that stick with me to this day.

My sister and I were fortunate. Our mother was strong — and smart — and saw to it that our lives were disrupted as little as possible after his death. She kept us on the straight and narrow, kept our household together and made sure that both of us attended college. She made sure that education continued to be important in our family. I'll always be grateful to her for that.

But nothing could lessen the pain that I felt when my father died.

I thought of all the things that we'd done together — kite flying, tossing a ball in the backyard, fishing in Forest Park. I thought about how we'd go to ballgames together when I received *Post-Dispatch* "Straight-A" tickets to see the Cardinals at Busch Stadium. I thought about the piggyback rides he used to give me when I was younger.

To this day, I think about the things that we did together. And then I wish desperately that he was still here.

How I'd love to have him back — if only for half an hour — to seek his advice, ask him questions, tell him what I've done and give him a big hug.

My dad was always interested in current events, and he paid close attention to the news. I'd love to have discussions with him today about presidential politics, the Rodney King issue, the South Africa situation and other issues in the news. On occasion, I've even had dreams about him coming back.

And I find myself on occasion wondering how my life may have differed had he lived. Would I have gone to the same college? Would I have become a journalist? Would I have been a different kind of father?

And I wish that my dad had had the opportunity to meet my son. He's 11 years old and, in many ways, reminds me of myself at that age. I often tell William what his grandfather was like, but I'd give anything for them to be able to meet just once.

I suppose no matter how old one gets to be, one never really gets over the death of a parent.

And that's why those who do still have their fathers today should consider themselves fortunate.

Because when they're gone, they're gone, and life is much different.

My wife and son have plans for me today, and I am proud to be a father. I hope that I am doing everything that I can to be a good father to my son.

But I also wish that I had someone to wish a happy father's day to today as well.

Someone I could thank for all of his efforts to raise me right, to teach me a work ethic, to do so many things with me that I have the pleasant memories of him that I have today.

To those who still have their fathers, cherish them — not just today, Father's Day, but every day. We often don't value our parents nearly enough until they're gone.

And then, of course, it's too late.

I miss you, Dad. *(June 21, 1992)*

GREAT ISSUES: POTATO SALAD, RIBS AND BEER

Call it the potato salad faux pas.

That's what I call a "debate" concerning an upcoming family reunion.

I'm a member of a small committee of family members putting our reunion together. It's a big deal in our family, since the last one of these we held was about eight years ago.

At a recent meeting, we began a discussion about the menu for this event, for which we're expecting as many as 100 people.

One person made the mistake of volunteering to buy potato salad.

The meeting erupted.

"Store-bought potato salad!" sniffed one family member. "I can't believe you suggested store-bought potato salad."

"That's for sure," harrumphed another. "It doesn't taste right. I always make my potato salad myself."

The member who had suggested buying the potato salad tried to explain herself. "I just thought that we could save a lot of time and effort if we just bought it . . . ."

"Oh, no," someone else said. "What's the point in having a family picnic if the food's no good?"

"You know, they fly that potato salad into the stores frozen and then they thaw it out," contributed another.

"It's frozen?" shrieked one member, in absolute horror. "Good Lord, that's awful!"

This conversation went on and on for a good 20 minutes, and I wondered if we were going to have a food fight — literally. Finally, the poor woman who had suggested buying the potato salad decided that her life would be worth living only if she withdrew her suggestion, and several people volunteered to make the potato salad instead.

Things were going smoothly again until the menu discussion turned to meat. The reunion's chief planners had said that we would have barbecued ribs, riblets, rib tips, chicken wings and chicken breasts.

Maybe there's something in me that likes living dangerously. Anyway, I made the innocent mistake of suggesting that perhaps we had too much meat. "Since we'll have riblets and rib tips, why don't we drop the ribs?" I suggested. "We could save a lot of money that we could put to use elsewhere."

I looked over at my mother and knew I was in trouble when I saw her jaw drop.

"No ribs?" she asked, incredulously. "I don't think it's much of a picnic without ribs."

"I just thought that since we had all that other meat, that we could cut back by dropping the ribs," I said.

"Well, do what you want to do," my mother said, in that voice that says that her only son is doing something terribly stupid and she can't understand why.

That sparked 25 more minutes of debate. To rib or not to rib? That was the question.

The answer was to rib, after all. My mother won out.

Needless to say, these family meetings last for several hours. This particular one lasted 3 1/2 hours. We always manage to get things done, but it sometimes takes a while to get to it.

Like when we discussed how much beer to buy for the reunion weekend which, in addition to the picnic, will include several other events.

Some thought that 40 packs of beer would be a good amount to have.

Others of us thought that was a bit high.

"Everyone's not going to drink beer," I suggested.

"That's true," said someone else, backing me up. "Plus, we don't want people to get drunk. You know, we have some relatives who will drink as long as they can stand up."

Others disagreed. "I don't think 40 packs is too much,"

one said. "It's going to be hot during the picnic, and people are going to want to drink to keep cool."

"But that's the whole point," said one committee member. "We don't want them drinking lots of beer to cool off. That's why we're buying plenty of soda."

"That may be so, but some people won't want to drink soda. We don't want people getting angry because there's not enough beer."

That incensed one relative. "Well, if they get angry, they can run out and buy some more themselves. This isn't a bar, it's a picnic. What do people expect?"

You guessed it: Another half-hour discussion before a decision to buy 30 packs of beer instead.

After months of planning, the reunion's coming up this weekend. Those of us on the committee are finally beginning to smile as we watch it fall into place.

But I must admit I'll feel a certain emptiness when this weekend's over.

Who am I going to argue with now? *(July 30, 1993)*

IT'S TOUGH TO SAY GOODBYE TO A HOME THAT SO REFLECTS US

This is it. The boxes are mostly packed, the moving company's been notified, and the new place is ready for us to move in.

Moving day comes this week. We're leaving our St. Louis home of 17 years. The muscular dystrophy that I've developed in recent years makes it too difficult for me to go up and down the steps. So we're moving to a one-story condo, also in the city.

It's not easy leaving this old house. So many memories were made here. Will's first bike. The many Thanksgiving and Christmas dinners, the many Mother's Days and Father's

Days. The magical times when Will was so full of excitement he would wake up at 3 a.m. to look for his presents under the Christmas tree. The bevy of dogs and cats who endeared themselves as part of our lives over the years. The special evening that we took pictures of Will and his prom date on the wooden staircase, a photo in which he looked just like my late father.

The house on the street with the funny name that no one could ever pronounce or spell: DeGiverville. The words, "That's D-e-G-i-v-e-r-v-i-l-l-e," were regularly heard whenever one of us was on the phone.

One memory that endures is my Fourth of July barbecue. I had hung our American flag from the front porch. As I grilled steaks and basted ribs, the wind suddenly kicked up, and rain started to pour. The next thing I knew, my flag was soaring past me, down the alley, leaving me to run and retrieve it in the downpour. Another memory that comes to mind was eight years ago, when we hosted a Mexican family of seven at our home. Some members of the family, who were friends of ours, spoke only Spanish, so Spanish was heard throughout the 10 days they were here. The only television channel that played was Univision, the Spanish-speaking cable network. The house was packed, and the visit drove my wife, Elizabeth — who understands Spanish but doesn't speak it — up the wall.

When we bought the house, we thought that it would be the home we would get old in, maybe retire in. We loved the two-story home with its sturdy, colonial-style columns in front, its liberal use of wood throughout the interior, its gorgeous staircase, its leaded glass windows, its 1916 construction. We could imagine this area when it was built. Only 12 years after the World's Fair, there probably wasn't much here at the time. The fair probably was a major asset in developing the area around it.

We always thought the house was in a terrific location,

too. Walking distance from Forest Park, just a stone's throw from the History Museum. Less than a block away from a MetroLink stop. And being part of the Skinker-DeBaliviere neighborhood made us part of a community steeped in tradition, a neighborhood that is diverse, both racially and economically.

We put a lot of loving care into this old house over the years. We installed ceiling fans in every room. We updated the kitchen and installed a dishwasher, one that Elizabeth swore she would never need, and later couldn't live without. We adorned the living room walls with new wallpaper. We painted the mustard yellow dining room white. We built a deck in the back yard, and added a privacy fence. We added outdoor lighting. We redid the bathroom, got rid of the old claw-foot tub and added a shower. The house reflects us.

In many ways, the house today is so much better than it was when we moved here. Of course, the new residents will surely look at the place, scratch their heads about why we did this or that, and make plenty of changes over time as well. They may update the kitchen again, redo the deck, change the wallpaper, choose a color other than white for the bedrooms. They'll surely make the house reflect them. That's how houses evolve.

So while our wallpaper, our dishwasher, our ceiling fans and our bathroom will all go with the house, our memories won't. Those we'll take with us.

Meanwhile, the new place we're moving into is very nice. It has many amenities that our house didn't: central air conditioning, for instance; a parking garage; and more than one bathroom. The carpeted floors will be nice too. At the new place, we'll surely gather countless new memories.

But we'll always cherish the old. *(May 19, 2002)*

IF CHITLINS AREN'T ON YOUR TURKEY DAY MENU, IT'S NOT A REAL HOLIDAY

While some of you are preparing for a mouth-watering turkey this Thanksgiving, my mouth is preparing for something entirely different: chitterlings.

They're pronounced chitlins really, unless you're the formal type. Then look for raised eyebrows when you say "chitter-lings."

I've been eating chitterlings since I can remember, and I love 'em. They're no health food by any stretch of the imagination, and they're certainly not on my diet. But since I eat them maybe once a year, I figure it's OK to take the chance.

Hard as it is for me to believe, some people have never tasted chitterlings. Some have never even heard of them. Unlike calamari, a word someone decided looked better on a menu than the word squid, chitterlings don't hide behind a nice, trendy name. They are, put bluntly, the small intestines of a pig.

Don't sound particularly appetizing? Maybe you haven't tasted them. All right, maybe you have. Chitterlings are the kind of food people love or hate.

When I grew up, holiday meals on Thanksgiving and Christmas weren't the same without chitterlings with Louisiana hot sauce, ham, a carved turkey, macaroni and cheese, collard greens and sweet potato pie for dessert. My mother cooked the best chitterlings, bar none. She still does. So on Thursday, she's preparing Thanksgiving dinner, which will include the requisite chitterlings.

You don't just eat chitterlings, though. They require cleaning.

It takes some real work to clean chitterlings. The preparer can spend several hours pulling the fat away from the meat. Chitterlings that aren't cleaned properly can cause a bacterial infection called yersiniosis. But before you say "A-ha, that's why I don't eat chitterlings," consider that yersiniosis can also come from other foods, including shellfish, tofu, ice cream and milk.

Some stores have started carrying pre-cleaned chitterlings, but most chitterling purists turn their noses up at them (and it's not just because of the smell). It's always best to clean your own chitterlings, they insist. Quality control, you know.

After cleaning, chitterlings are put on for a long boil, often with hog maws, a little vinegar and salt and pepper.

Chitterlings aren't known for having a great smell when they're cooking, so some people toss in a potato or an apple to help absorb some of the odor. But the smell is worth it once you take your first bite.

Some people choose to bread chitterlings and then fry them. There's even a chain of restaurants in Atlanta where you can drive up and order fried chitterlings with french fries and cole slaw.

Some African-Americans are offended by chitterlings because they were eaten by slaves in the Old South because their white masters got the best parts of the pork. The idea that blacks had to eat leftover parts like chitterlings is, to some, demeaning.

Because of that, I know some black folks who are closet chitterling eaters. They love them but don't want people to know; they would never order them in a restaurant. Yet chitterlings are a part of African-American history, or at least in the South. In other parts of the country, blacks prepared and ate different foods altogether.

For years, I'd thought that chitterlings were strictly a soul food, something eaten only by African-Americans. I later learned that chitterlings are also popular among many Southern whites, who consider them part of Southern cooking.

They're also part of Cajun cooking. That andouille sausage that you like so well? That heavily smoked sausage is made from chitterlings and tripe.

It's not just Americans who are eating chitterlings. I've known for years that chitterlings are eaten in Mexico in a spicy, tomato-based soup. But more research found that chitterlings are truly international. In Hungary, I found, chitterlings are used for cases and as stuffing for sausages. Chitterling sausages are also a delicacy in France. And chitterlings can be found in certain Asian dishes.

So while you're slicing that turkey or ham this Thanksgiving, think about me, diving into a plate of chitterlings with all the trimmings.

Pass the hot sauce, please. *(Nov. 26, 1996)*

SOMETIMES WE NEED TO BE REMINDED OF THE BLESSINGS AROUND US

During a class after church on Sunday, our group listened to a song recorded by a young man.

In a clear, strong and pleasant voice, he sang about all the things that he was thankful for: He sang of the sounds of birds, the joy of nature, the feeling of raindrops.

When the song ended, Donna, who led our group, explained that the singer was only 23 and studying to become a priest when he died last year of leukemia. Despite his illness, he remained thankful for so much.

The song and story struck me. How many times have I complained about things, without realizing that I really have much to be thankful for?

Today, Thanksgiving Day, seems an appropriate time to take stock of all that I really am thankful for.

I am thankful for nature.

Like the young man who was studying to become a priest,

I appreciate nature. I take it for granted far too often. But the sensation of a gentle rain cascading on my face, the feel of a slight wind caressing my skin, the sound of rustling leaves on a clear, dry day — I love them all.

They remind me that the world is a much bigger place than I can even imagine. They remind me that despite all of the bad things that go on in the world, there are plenty of good ones as well.

I am thankful for not being hungry.

Like most Americans, I'm overweight. I dream of being thinner; of having a body that would make women swoon and men jealous.

Still, I'm thankful for never having to go to bed hungry, as millions do each night. I'm thankful that I've never had to stand in line for handouts of food, or had to feel my stomach bloated, not because of too much food, but because of too little.

I am thankful for life.

Some of you followed my progress earlier this year as I learned that I had prostate cancer and subsequently underwent prostate surgery. When I first learned that I had cancer, my first thought was that I was going to die.

But I didn't. The surgery went well, my doctors were excellent, and my prayers were answered. I survived, and I continue to get better, day by day. I'm thankful that my life has gone on. And I'm thankful that the most recent tests have shown that the cancer is gone, hopefully never to return.

I am thankful for my health.

I'm not as healthy as I'd like to be. But I am able to walk, to move my arms and legs, to speak in a normal voice, to use my brain, my eyes, my ears. I realize that everyone is not as fortunate.

I am thankful for my family.

I don't think I've ever appreciated my family more than I do now. Perhaps it's perspective that comes with the graying of my hair, but I've begun to value my family more than ever before. I am grateful for my wife, who has had to put up with me, bad habits and all, for 20 years of marriage. I am grateful for my son, who's trying to find his own way in the world now as a college student and who has had to put up with an overachiever for a dad, and the trials and tribulations that go with that.

I'm grateful for my mother who, to this day, encourages me and shares my times of greatest triumph as willingly as she shares my moments of deepest despair. Without her guidance and strength, I could never have done many of the things I've done in life. Without her, my life today would have been quite different.

I'm grateful for my sister and brother-in-law, who often share with me different ways of looking at things. I've learned much over the years by looking at issues from other perspectives and, without knowing it, they've been instrumental in helping me do that.

There is so much that I have to be thankful for. And while I've chosen today to pause and think about them, I realize that I should be just as thankful on the other 364 days of the year as well. *(Nov. 25, 1999)*

OUR HOLIDAY FOOD FIGHT ALWAYS ENDS SWEETLY, WITH SOMETHING FOR EVERYONE

It's getting to be Christmastime around the Freeman household, and that can mean only one thing: food fight. Not food fight in the John Belushi, "Animal House" kind of way. No, I'm talking about what we're eating.

It's a very big deal for us. I imagine there are many folks who decide a week or so before Christmas what the meal will be. You've got to make plans so you can be sure to have all the ingredients you need to make the meal.

Not so in our household. The minute Thanksgiving is over, we go to work on planning the Christmas dinner. For instance, there's always the fruitcake question. I love fruitcake. I always have, dating back to when I was a little boy and my family had it every year. My wife, on the other hand, can't stand the stuff. She thinks fruitcakes are made to be doorstops, bookends, bricks — anything but something that anyone would want to eat.

In recent years, I've been ordering fruitcakes made by monks. They're really quite good and they preserve well. Unfortunately, this year I forgot to order the fruitcake, so my wife is gloating, thrilled that there will be no fruitcake to kick around this Christmas.

On the other hand, we will be having the traditional Freeman family eggnog. This eggnog recipe was created by my grandfather. My father made it, I've made it, and now our son, Will, makes it. Unfortunately, there are a couple of problems with the recipe. First, it calls for a tiny bit of Scotch, to help kick in the flavor. Every year, when we make the eggnog, my mother never thinks there's enough Scotch in it. She's not a big drinker, but she says there's not enough to wake up the flavor. I, on the other hand, think that more Scotch would not only wake up the flavor but the neighbors next door as well. So that's one of our battles.

Second, my wife doesn't like eggnog. I seem to recall her pretending to like it when we were dating, but she says that my memory's fuzzy, so who knows? Her memory is always better than mine, so I guess I'll have to go along.

Then come the meats. Turkey is standard — or at least with most of us. For me, turkey is a must on Christmas and Thanksgiving. Other meats can come or go, but you've got to have a turkey, as far as I'm concerned. My wife stirred things up a few years ago when she suggested that instead of turkey, we have a nice lasagna for Christmas. Will and I were shocked. Lasagna? On Christmas? That was downright blasphemy. She quickly took that suggestion off the table, and we calmed down.

In recent years, we've been getting Honey Baked hams for the holidays. These hams are so sweet and smoky, they don't compare to other hams, in our opinion. So no one will fight over that. But then comes another item that always causes a little controversy: chitterlings.

Some folks can't stand them. Not me. I love them, dotted with Louisiana hot sauce.

They're the best. But my wife doesn't care for them. Never has, she says, although I remember once when we were dating when she ate them and talked about how good they were. I now know she was just being polite. So not only won't she eat them, she won't cook them. Fortunately, my mother will make those and bring them to dinner. Will enjoys them too, so they'll be eaten.

Finally comes the dessert and the annual battle of the pies. The question? Pumpkin or sweet potato? It should be easy to decide. One or the other. Maybe in another household, but not ours. I like both sweet potato pies and pumpkin pies. So does Will. However, my mother likes sweet potato pies and doesn't like pumpkin. My wife loves pumpkin pies and doesn't care for sweet potato. While it's not quite Oscar Madison-Felix Ungar time ("Can two divorced men share an apartment without driving each other crazy?"), it often means working something out. We've tried things like having apple pie instead, but that doesn't seem to please anyone. So come Christmas, we'll have both pumpkin and sweet potato pie.

Despite all the wrangling, the fighting and the battling,

family and friends will still gather around at Christmas and enjoy dinner. The only fighting then will be over who gets to do the dishes. *(Dec. 22, 2002)*

CAT'S ILLNESS LETS HIS LOVE FOR FELINES OUT OF THE BAG

It's 2 A.M., and one of our three cats is having some sort of seizure.

I'm not sure what to do, so I pick him up and hold him in my arms to try to calm him.

These little seizures have been going on for a couple of weeks, and the vet doesn't yet know what's causing them.

What we do know is that the cat is 14 years old and is having kidney problems. He's eating special food and we're giving him medication to deal with an infection. The vet also has given him several shots and has monitored him several times. We're hoping he pulls through.

Now I don't really consider myself a cat person. I'm much more of a dog person. I had two dogs when I was growing up. Scrappy was my favorite. He was part cocker spaniel, part mutt, and I loved him. We got him when I was about 8. He finally died when I was 21.

My wife, on the other hand, was always a cat person. When she and I first met, she and her father had a cat named Kiki. Kiki never liked me. She'd always hiss at me anytime I'd get close. I always thought it was because she knew that someday I'd take Elizabeth away from her.

The difference between dogs and cats is like the difference between pigs and cows: they've both got four legs and a tail, but the similarities end there.

For me, dogs are much more lovable. They come immediately when you call them, unlike most cats I know. When dogs see you, they're excited and their tails wag with enthusiasm.

Cats may be excited when they see you as well, but they're too cool to let you know. You can call their names until your vocal chords are swollen and they may never come. If you're lucky, they may saunter over to you and let you pet them.

Dogs love to lick your hands and your face to say hello. Not only do cats not do this, but their tongues are like sandpaper. Being licked by a cat wouldn't necessarily be a good experience.

And we won't even discuss the issue of cats and fur balls. Never saw one of those come from a dog.

After my wife and I got married, we talked about our pet passions, my love for dogs, hers for cats. In the end, she won out, mainly because we lived in an apartment where it would have been more difficult to keep a dog than a cat.

So we got Maxwell, a playful kitten who thought there was nothing on earth more fun than a balled-up wad of aluminum foil.

After owning Maxwell for a few years, we inherited Bullwinkle. He came from a friend. The friend, Roland, and his wife were moving to Nashville and were desperate to find a good owner for their two cats. My wife and I talked a long time about it. I was a bit reluctant to have two cats. But Elizabeth wanted him so, and Roland really needed someone to take their cats, so I relented. We took Bullwinkle. Someone else got Rocky.

Bullwinkle was different from Maxwell. Maxwell was wellbehaved. He'd always been an indoor cat. Bullwinkle, on the other hand, had always been an outdoor cat and was filled with energy. That was OK, except that we live in the city, and it didn't take too long for us to learn that Bullwinkle was going to have to live in the house. City streets are no place for a cat, at least not for Bullwinkle.

It took him a while for him to learn to calm down. But it took no time at all for him to become my son's favorite.

Will loved to play with Bullwinkle, and the cat loved to play with him. Will would make the cat jump for him. Bullwinkle was more fickle than Maxwell — although it seems to me that all cats are fickle — but Will was able to get him to come when he'd call him. Whenever I call for the cat, I find that I would have had better luck getting Elvis to come to me.

To this day, he prefers sleeping in Will's room to any other room in the house.

We've since inherited a third cat, Josephine, from my father-in-law. She has a very regal attitude about her, and I think she believes the people in the house are her subjects. She's finicky about what she eats and doesn't enjoy it when the other cats try to play with her. It musses her fur.

Bullwinkle remains Will's favorite, and while I'm not head over heels about any of the cats, I know how much my son loves this cat.

So on this particular night I cradle him in my arms as he shakes uncontrollably.

Come on, Bullwinkle, pull through. I say a little prayer for him and look at him, his feet moving back and forth.

The shaking lasts for only five minutes, but it seems like it's been five hours. Bullwinkle goes limp now, and I lay him on the living room rug and worry about him.

As I said, I'm not much of a cat person. But my son loves this cat.

That's reason enough for me to love him, too. *(March 18, 1997)*

HE DIDN'T SEEK FAME OR FORTUNE, BUT HIS FAMILY FELT HIS LOVE

William Dean Johnson was a gentle man.

Yes, a gentleman in the common sense of the word. He opened doors for women, waited for women to be seated before he sat and rarely had a cross word to say about others.

But he was a gentle man too. He lived a peaceful life. He didn't bother others. After his wife died, he raised his young daughter alone, serving as a perfect dad.

That gentle man died early Thanksgiving morning, at the age of 76. He was buried Monday.

He was my father-in-law.

Johnson — "Dad," as I came to call him after my wife and I married 19 years ago — was always kind to me. He was a man of few words, something I hadn't realized when I first met him, which made me wonder if he really liked me. Over time, though, I learned that he was not a person to carry on lengthy conversations.

My wife and I met when we were students at Washington University, both working for the school paper. The first time she brought me to her house, I wondered what he would say. I'm black; Elizabeth is white.

As it turns out, he said "hello" and "pleased to meet you."

He was always like that. Race seemed unimportant to him. When Elizabeth and I decided to marry, I wondered what he would think. No one in my wife's family had ever married a black man. I was smart enough to realize that it might be a real shock to the family.

But dad embraced me immediately. His kind, gentle nature shone through once again.

When he was growing up, though, Dad was the Johnson family's own Dennis the Menace, and family members sometimes told him so. Once, when he was about 5, he walked away from home, traveling several blocks, until he arrived at a barber shop at Union and Easton avenues, what is now known as Martin Luther King Drive.

He ambled into the barber shop, plopped into the barber chair and asked for a haircut.

The barber, amused by this little boy, asked his name.

"General," he replied.

"General?" the barber asked. "General what?"

"General Nuisance," he said.

The barber called the police, and the little nuisance was soon returned to his family.

The little boy grew up to be a handsome man. A black-and-white portrait of him, taken in the early 1950s, shows a striking young man with a calm, gentle expression. He married Mozelle DeLoach in 1946, and the two had a daughter. Together they raised the blond-haired little girl, until Mozelle died, when their only daughter was 12. Dad raised her into adulthood, spending hours and hours with her. At times he was more like a sibling than a father. Together they would go sledding, to the movies and on long walks. He loved to walk, sometimes making it hard for his daughter to keep up.

He worked for many years for a company that made restaurant equipment, putting together catalogs. But unlike some men, who find their greatest pleasure in their work, he found his in his family and in his hobbies. He liked singing and playing the guitar, and he had a good singing voice. He also played the harmonica and piano.

In later years, after his grandson was born, he taught him a couple of his bad habits, including opening a straw and blowing the paper wrapper off, and blowing on the tops of empty soda bottles to make noises.

He enjoyed cats. His first cat, Kiki, was a constant companion until her death. Later, Josephine, a regal cat from the

Gasconade pound, came into his life, developing a jealous relationship with him. When anyone else would kiss him on the cheek, Josephine would jump in his lap to divert his attention.

In his later years, his health began to fail, but he always remained in good spirits, enjoying classical music, Harrison Ford movies and National Geographic magazine.

He wasn't someone who was in the news. He was not a person who had, nor sought, fame or fortune. He was an ordinary man who was known by his daughter as an extraordinary father.

That extraordinary father died in his sleep Thursday, gently, just as he had lived. *(Dec. 1, 1998)*

FOLLOW THESE TIPS TO AVOID PITFALLS OF MOTHER'S DAY

OK, fellas, consider this your three-day warning.

Mother's Day is Sunday.

If you're like most guys, you haven't given it any thought. I know that until now, I've given it very little.

But you can be sure that your wife is watching. And your mother isn't far behind. At this moment, they're dreaming about what you're going to get for them.

It's got to be the right present, bar none. Anything less and you'll be telling Fido to move over Sunday night.

I've learned a few things about Mother's Day over the years. So, in the name of sharing and giving to my fellow man, here are:

Greg's Tips for Men on Mother's Day Gifts.

1. If she says, "You don't have to get me anything for Mother's Day," don't believe it. The words certainly sound tempting, don't they? But especially for those who are young and new husbands, trust me. I haven't been married for 21

years for nothing.

If you really want to disappoint your wife, agree with her that you don't have to get her a Mother's Day present. Mother's Day won't be a happy one for those in the household. And don't expect anything on Father's Day either.

2. Listen to your wife or mother when she tells you what she doesn't want for Mother's Day. My mother does this regularly. Don't get her another grooming kit, she'll say. She has enough of those. Don't get her a scarf because she has enough scarves. It might be easier selecting her gift by looking at what she doesn't want.

3. When it comes to greeting cards, don't use me as an example. This is my routine with greeting cards: The day before Mother's Day, I march into the store and head to the greeting card section. There, I do battle, elbowing my way through a crowd of men, all staring, zombie-like, at what's left in the card section as they mumble, "must . . . find . . . card."

Finally, I pick up one of the last cards remaining, a card with RuPaul's face on the front, and the words, "Have a mother of a day." Oh yeah. My mother will like that one.

4. Wives and mothers don't like getting gifts that aren't personal. While I once may have thought that a set of Teflon pots and pans would be ideal for my wife, I have since learned that such a present is likely to get the good-intentioned giver one across the lips, and I don't mean a kiss, either.

While I wouldn't object to getting a power saw for Father's Day, don't even think about doing the same for Mother's Day. As the old saying goes, that dog won't hunt.

5. The phrase, "It's the thought that counts," is applied to children, not husbands. If you're a child, a mangled bowl-like item that you make and give to your mother as an ashtray will be cherished on Mother's Day, even if dear old mom

doesn't smoke. It will become a lifelong keepsake.

But don't expect the same rules to apply if you're a husband. Cheap perfume or a chintzy, cut-glass ring won't cut the mustard. She'll wonder if your thoughts were cheap. Don't even go there.

6. If your wife isn't a mother, don't assume that you shouldn't get her a Mother's Day present. This is especially true for newlyweds. A disappointed wife who gets not even a card on Mother's Day is likely to ask why not, and the response that she's not a mother can easily draw a response like, "But I hope to be someday." That leaves you with your jaw dropped open after you say, "Duh!"

7. If you can't cook, don't start now. The worst thing you can do is to try to whip up dinner for her if the only thing you're used to cooking is a boiled egg. Chances are you'll come up with some concoction that neither you nor she will want to eat, and she'll inherit your dirty dishes. This is not the way to say I love you.

So there you have it, guys. A three-day warning and some tips to help you stay away from the potential minefields.

Don't say you weren't warned. *(May 11, 2000)*

IT'S HARD SAYING GOODBYE TO AN OLD FRIEND OF THE FAMILY

How do you say goodbye to a friend of 20 years?

My wife and I were faced with that question recently after our cat became very ill.

Maxwell had been our companion since a month after we married in 1979. He'd been a present to us from a former editor of the *Belleville News-Democrat*, where I worked at the time. My wife and I named him after a favorite restaurant in Belleville.

We brought the kitten home and found him to be lots of

fun. My wife had been the cat lover in the family; I had always had dogs when I was growing up.

So I trained Max like one would train a dog. He knew how to sit, how to lie down, how to jump, how to come when he was called. Cats have a reputation of doing whatever they want to do, so people were always amazed when Max would come running when I called him.

Max had his own oddities. He had a fear of large things. Once, when I had purchased a new headboard for our bed, he went ballistic. After I brought the headboard into the house, the cat vanished. I feared he'd darted out the door when I wasn't looking.

Finally, I heard a timid "meow" coming from behind the refrigerator. The cat had gone there to hide and was terrified. I brought him out, but he was still afraid.

I called the Humane Society for advice. Someone there suggested that we introduce him to the headboard. (I imagined saying something like, "Max, this is the headboard. Headboard, this is Max.") Eventually, he got used to it, but it took awhile.

Max was a smart cat as well. Apparently hungry one day while we were gone, he managed to open the refrigerator door. When we got home, we found the fridge open and a loaf of gnawed-upon French bread on the floor. It was clear that this wasn't your everyday cat.

Max could have been an art critic in a previous life. He liked to look at paintings. He'd stare at them, almost as if he were studying them, examining the subtle shades of gray, blue and green.

When our son came along, we learned of Max's patience. When Will was small, he would pull Max's tail, try to ride him, pick him up and toss him around and do all sorts of things that would stretch anyone's patience. But Max was tolerant, never tried to bite him or otherwise harm him.

His patience extended to two other cats who came into our possession over the years. Both of those cats loved to try to provoke Max, but usually to no avail. Max would protect himself, but usually refused to be drawn into the shenanigans. He was the Gandhi of cats.

Over the years, the other cats died, but Max hung in there with us. He began getting afflictions common with age — a touch of arthritis and difficulty hearing — but he got around fairly well.

In recent weeks, though, he got ill. He couldn't control his bowels. He became lethargic. He lost his hunger — even his love for chicken, always a favorite.

My wife took him to the vet, who gave her some medication with nutrients to make sure he got the vitamins he needed.

That didn't help much, and finally we knew that we could no longer keep the cat. But it was difficult for us to decide what to do. We weren't sure we had the heart to put him to sleep. I briefly explored the idea of finding a shelter that doesn't kill animals. Maybe he could live there until his death, I thought.

But our son was against that. He feared that after all the years Max had lived with us, he'd be traumatized by being in a new environment. He would die thinking we didn't love him, Will reasoned.

Finally, we decided: Max would have to be put to sleep. My wife called the vet and made an appointment for 1 p.m. on a recent Saturday.

But Max had other ideas: He died with my wife at his side at 10:30 that morning.

I never knew how much I'd miss him — me, the dog person and all. But I've even dreamed about him a couple of times.

It's really hard to lose an old friend. *(Nov. 2, 1999)*

SINCE THANKSGIVING WAS SO NICE, WHY NOT HAVE IT TWICE?

Longing for leftovers.

What do you do if you really enjoy Thanksgiving?

In my case, you celebrate it again.

Like most Americans, my wife, Elizabeth, and I celebrated Thanksgiving two weeks ago. It was a family affair. My mother came to our home for dinner. Our son Will, 19, came home from college to join us.

Family activities these days often have something to do with Will's hair. He's growing dreadlocks. Though it's taken me a while, I've gotten used to his hair. Partly because when I was his age, I did what I wanted with my hair, despite my mother's protests; partly because I know that he's at school in Chicago and I'm here, so there's not much I can do about it anyway. When it comes to hair, however, my mother hasn't changed her tune. She usually has a few words to say to him about his hair like, "When are you going to cut that stuff off?"

This time, though, there was none of that; just a peaceful day with family. We talked about life in Chicago, where Will's attending school; about the presidential campaign that refused to die; about other relatives. We took pictures and used the good china to serve the traditional Thanksgiving dinner: turkey and dressing, cranberry sauce, mashed potatoes with gravy, green beans, and for dessert, apple and sweet potato pies and ice cream.

A big meal, to put it mildly.

After dinner — and before I fell into a tryptophan stupor — we sent a plate of food home with my mother, and she took another plate of food for a friend. When Will left, we sent him with helpings of turkey, dressing and dessert.

So unlike some folks, who found themselves the week after Thanksgiving eating turkey sandwiches, turkey soup, turkey pot pies, you name it, we had no turkey left over. The Freemans had taken care of it all.

At first, we thought that was a great idea. We'd gotten rid of our leftovers. There were no containers with a little bit of this or that in the refrigerator. At the end of Thanksgiving night, it was over, and that was that.

But then last week, my wife and I talked about our meal. It seemed especially good this year. Even my mother, who's no slouch in the kitchen herself, told my wife that this was the best Thanksgiving dinner she'd prepared yet. "You really put your foot in it this year," my mother said, complimenting Elizabeth.

We really enjoyed the holiday, we thought, and began lamenting that none of that Thanksgiving dinner was left. We kept talking and came up with the same idea at the same time. Since Thanksgiving was so nice, why not do it twice?

Off we went, to buy another turkey. After picking up a good-sized bird, Elizabeth cooked it for several hours late last week until it was a juicy, delicate, golden brown.

It wasn't terribly practical to try to bring the whole family together again for this meal — sending for our son to come home from Chicago again last week just so we could celebrate Thanksgiving once more didn't seem like the best idea — so this time it was just the two of us.

Not only did we sit down to another delicious turkey dinner, we also had gravy, dressing and the works to go with it. This time we served corn with dinner, and Jello for dessert. We even used the good china again. And once more, it was a good meal. Tryptophan heaven once again.

Even better, this time we've got leftovers. In no time I'm

sure that we'll be eating turkey soup, turkey sandwiches and turkey pot pie. And there will be no complaints from me.

In fact, this idea of celebrating a holiday twice reminds me that we have another holiday coming up soon.

I wonder how difficult it would be to celebrate Christmas twice? *(Dec. 5, 2000)*

FROM LONG HAIR TO MAC AND CHEESE, SOME THINGS BRIDGE GENERATIONS

The "heir" is once again apparent.

It's been a noisy week at the Freeman household.

The "heir" is home.

Our son Will is home from college — at least for a short while. He's headed back to Chicago this summer to work and take a class. But he's taken a brief respite from the Windy City and landed in the Gateway City, and my wife and I are glad to see him.

Suddenly the CD player — the one I practically need a manual to operate — is getting plenty of use, with songs that I never heard of. The opinions about music are flowing, from Britney Spears ("No way!" "Overexposed!") to the Skatalites ("They rock!"). The phone is ringing more often these days, and the calls are almost always for Will.

He looks thinner than he did when we sent him to Chicago. From what he's told us, that should come as no surprise. The idea of a balanced meal apparently flew out the window at college. He and his roommates lived on staples such as ramen noodles and macaroni and cheese.

Of course, macaroni and cheese reminded me of my own college days. In those days, you could get four boxes of Kraft macaroni and cheese for a dollar. For a couple of bucks, I could have dinner for a week. Not the most nutritious, mind you — I guess it would have been nice to have eaten items such as vegetables and fruit — but I survived.

And Will has survived, seemingly no worse from the rigors of college. He somehow seems older, more mature. And not just because of the mustache and goatee that he's sprouted since high school. He seems more responsible. College has done good things for him.

He had a good school year, too. He hasn't gotten his second-semester grades back yet, but he thinks he did pretty well. And he did well during his first semester, as well. Freshman year can be a real shock to the system for some students — it certainly was for me — but he seems to have adapted remarkably well.

Meanwhile, I've promised myself to say very little about his long hair, which, he says, he is growing into dreadlocks. I'm doing my best not to become one of those grouchy parents who gripes all the time, "You kids! With the hair and the music!"

So far, I've remained pretty calm about it, which is less than my mother did when I was in college and grew a big Afro. I look back now at some of the pictures of myself during that time and laugh. Maybe a time will come when Will will do the same. Meanwhile, I'll just have to grin and bear it.

Likewise, I'll have to grin and bear my continuing status as First National Bank of Dad. Between spending money and sending money, there must be banks with fewer withdrawals. It goes with being the parent of a college student, though. No one wants their child to starve to death. So I've spent the year writing checks. While writing checks isn't my favorite thing in the world (Will has apparently told people that I'm notoriously cheap), it's still worth it to support him, if only for the hope that some day, years from now, he won't put us in a home.

At times, it's amazing for me to realize that I'm the father of a college student.

It hardly seems possible. It seems like only yesterday that I was a college student myself. My wife and I met in college, working for the school paper. Was it really that long ago? Aren't we still part of "the Pepsi generation"? Aren't we still "kinda young, kinda now"?

I'd like to think so, but Will, who I think views his parents as kind and well-meaning but hopelessly behind the times, would surely disagree.

Even the commercials for the products that used to target us — soft drinks, fast food, shampoo and the like — now pretty much ignore us. How many people with salt-and-pepper hair have you seen in a shampoo commercial lately?

The future is in the hands of people like my son. I must say that those are pretty good hands. *(June 11, 2000)*

Greg Freeman: A Gentleman, A Gentle Man

Part 3:

Harmony

A CRIME AND AN ASSUMPTION: WHY THIS BLACK MAN IS ANGRY

As I watched the news unfold about the Washington University student who was abducted and killed, I found myself making a familiar plea:

Oh God, don't let the suspects be black.

As time went on, I found that God had chosen not to answer my prayer; the suspects are, indeed, black.

I don't know the suspects. They don't work with me. I know that they're not my neighbors nor are they my relatives.

But I also know that every time a black person is involved in a murder, an entire race is indicted.

I don't exaggerate. More than my white colleagues, I suspect, I regularly receive hate mail from people who blame me for the atrocities that have been committed by others of my race.

An example of that are these words, from an anonymous postcard:

"Why don't you do something about your people killing everybody? Blacks are the scourge of this country."

I doubt that my white colleagues get letters telling them that they ought to do something about people like Susan Smith killing innocent children. Unfortunately, though, our society has a tendency to blame an entire group for the actions of even a small minority.

Indeed, black males who murder are a small minority. Most African-Americans are like everyone else — hard-working people who would like to live their lives in peace. And I know many who repeat the all-too-frequent refrain when reading the news:

Oh God, don't let the suspects be black.

Why should I even care about their color?

Probably because society regularly reminds me of mine, and I know that a few more non-blacks will look upon me suspiciously or even with animosity because of something I had nothing to do with. No matter what I do, no matter how I try to live a decent life, I'm regularly reminded of my color.

When I'm followed around in a department store when someone of a different color isn't, I'm reminded that I'm "different."

When I'm looked upon suspiciously when I go into certain neighborhoods, I'm reminded that I'm "different."

When a white woman clutches her purse as I go by as if I were going to try to snatch it, I'm reminded that I'm "different."

It really doesn't matter what I wear, what I do or how I live my life. Just recently, Earl Graves Jr., a businessman and senior vice president for Black Enterprise magazine, was accosted on a train by New York police officers while reading the paper and sipping orange juice. They relieved him of his briefcase and frisked him from top to bottom, looking for a weapon. Why? They told him they were looking for a black man with short hair who, they had been told, had been carrying a gun. A description like that, of course, would fit more than a million people in New York.

When this sort of thing happens to someone like Graves, what is any other black person to think?

None of this is to say that I want to be considered a victim. I'm not a victim, and don't want to be treated that way. What I do want, though, is for people to know that I grieve as much as anyone else for the Washington University student who was killed and that my heart goes out to the young woman who survived. As much as anyone, I want to see justice done to the low-lifes who did it.

I want people to know that I care just as much about the crime that's going on as anyone else. To me, it doesn't matter whether the crimes are being committed by blacks or whites, or against blacks or whites. What does matter is that the crime is going on at all. I am appalled at those who pass themselves off as human beings while committing such vicious and brutal crimes. (To be a human being means to have some humanity, and scum that commit these kinds of crimes, drive-by shootings and the like, clearly have none.)

I also want people to know that while I realize that there are various factors that must be taken into consideration when trying to analyze today's violent times, I don't think criminals can be excused for violence because of their upbringing. It's not right, of course, but I can understand someone stealing food because he can't feed his family. I've got no compassion for someone who kills people — for whatever reason. I don't want to hear about racism or poverty or anything else. I don't buy it.

But I also want people to realize that there are a good number of African-Americans out here — a majority of us, in fact — who are incensed by both the racism that lets some people assume that most of us are criminals, and by the crime that's taunting all of us.

Today I am an angry black man. *(May 12, 1995)*

CEREMONY MARKS 'SCENES OF HORROR' BURIED IN AREA'S MEMORY

The temperature was a chilly 46 degrees at 7 a.m. Saturday as about 100 people gathered near the East St. Louis riverfront.

Poet-critic Eugene B. Redmond pointed to the Mississippi River as he recited a poem about the "river of bones and flesh and blood."

A spirited group of men in African garb pounded drums with their hands at speeds that made them impossible to follow.

Bishop Michael Bates, pastor of the Word Harvest Full Gospel Baptist Church in St. Louis, told the gathering that "if a man doesn't know from whence he comes, he certainly doesn't know where he's going."

Kofi Maalik of Chicago performed a colorful African ceremony giving nourishment of water and food "to free the souls of the ancestors killed in 1917."

The gathering was part of a black political convention being held here this weekend. Organizers of the convention felt it was important for their delegates — many of whom are not from St. Louis — to understand what happened here nearly 80 years ago.

They'd be surprised to learn how many St. Louisans don't know what happened either.

In 1917, gangs of whites terrorized blacks in East St. Louis, killing at least 39, forcing thousands to flee and causing those blacks with jobs in the city to return only under special precautions.

It was in that year that the Aluminum Ore Co. hired thousands of blacks from the rural South as replacements for white workers who had gone out on strike. Employers in a variety of industries found that the blacks would work more cheaply than whites, and many displaced their white workers with black ones.

The result was legions of white families who went hungry because their chief breadwinners had lost their jobs. But it wasn't easy for the blacks either, whose numbers overwhelmed the city's employment opportunities. Those who were fortunate enough to find work often found themselves living in hovels, earning less than in the jobs they'd left behind in the South.

On the night of July 1, 1917, a Ford automobile drove through a black neighborhood, terrorizing residents as the car's occupants fired guns indiscriminately. No one was injured, but a black crowd assembled to the calling of church bells that night. A police car arrived, and the group immediately opened fire on it, killing two white officers inside. No one knows whether the intention was to kill police officers. Some suggest that because the police car was a Ford like the one that had terrorized the neighborhood, angry residents might not have known the difference.

Regardless, the shootings caused a bloody riot the next day, as mobs of whites ripped into black neighborhoods, torturing, beating and shooting black men, women and children. In some cases, homes of blacks were set ablaze while whites with guns waited to shoot the occupants who fled.

Some blacks were set afire; others were hanged. The murders were carried out randomly; in one case, a black St. Louis family was returning home from a fishing trip when they were attacked. The mob killed a 14-year-old boy and his father and scalped his mother.

East St. Louis was a city on fire.

At the end of the day, 47 people were reported dead — 39 black, eight white. More than 240 buildings and 44 rail cars were destroyed by fire. The damage was estimated at $500,000, more than $2.5 million in today's dollars.

Reports indicate that about 300 National Guardsmen arrived early during the riot, but in some instances they turned against the blacks, as did many police officers.

According to the 1918 report of a congressional investigating committee, "Scenes of horror that would have shocked a savage were viewed with placid unconcern by hundreds, whose hearts knew no pity and who seemed to revel in the feast of blood and cruelty."

Terrorized blacks fled the city in thousands. The congressional report said: "The fright of the (black) laborers went to such an extent — and it was fully justified by existing conditions — that special means of transportation had to be provided for them back and forth between St. Louis and East St. Louis in order to get them to work at all."

More than 21 people were arrested, though only 21 ever went to the penitentiary for their crimes: nine whites and 12 blacks.

The riot was a low point in this area's history.

It was against that backdrop that those killed were honored Saturday morning, in a dignified remembrance of the senseless murders of 1917. *(Sept. 29, 1996)*

BROTHAS, LET'S UNITE — AGAINST VIOLENCE, IRRESPONSIBLE SEX

Today's column is written for the African-American men. You don't have to turn away if you're not a black man, but brothas, this one's for you.

I don't know if you've checked lately, but we — black men — have an image problem.

Lots of people are afraid of us. Even Jesse Jackson has said that he would be worried if he were on the street at night and was approached by a young black man. Folks avoid us; "profiling" police officers target us.

Of course, it's only a minority of us who are involved in activities that are causing this fear. Most of us are honest folk, people who are going about our lives, doing our jobs, taking care of our families. Robbing someone is the furthest thing from our minds. We wouldn't think of shooting somebody simply because we had a disagreement.

But the rest of you are causing problems for all of us. The fear of us, while pretty irrational, isn't baseless. Take a look at the crimes in the St. Louis area. An overwhelming majority of those are black-on-black crimes. In fact, though some whites are afraid they'll be harmed by black males, statistics say otherwise: The most likely victim of a murder is a black man, killed by another black man. Regardless of how racist this world might be, no white person has made a black man shoot and kill another black man.

Brothas, we've got to learn how to settle our disputes in ways other than blowing folks away. Those of you who are doing that stuff have no idea how much better our lives would be if we could get away from this whole violence thing.

Your behavior is unacceptable. And it's time for the rest of us to stop tolerating it.

And while we're talking about not tolerating things, there's something else we've got to stop tolerating: impregnating young women out of wedlock.

An increasing number of young black men are having two, three, even four children out of wedlock by different mothers. Nearly three out of four black babies are born out of wedlock to mothers who are young and poor.

Some of you mistakenly think that this is an issue of manhood. You're wrong. The ability to be responsible for yourself and for others is what sets a man apart from other species.

If you're not ready to settle down and help raise a baby in

a healthy and stable household, you're not ready to be a father. Instead, you're causing more problems, including problems for the child you've created. That's because kids of single mothers are more likely to live in poverty than those who live with both of their parents. And black youngsters are five times more likely to live in poverty.

Yes, I know that young women have a responsibility in this area, too, but today's column isn't for them. It's for us.

If you're not ready to be a father — a real father who takes care of his kids and has the ability to support them — then the responsible thing to do is to either abstain or to use protection.

As black men, we've got to rise above the statistics. We've got to be strong and determined to defeat the racism in our lives, and part of that includes living productive lives and making sure that our children are born into a family ready to give them every opportunity possible.

You and I know that black men aren't nearly as terrible as we're sometimes made out to be. But there are steps that we can take — that we have to take — to erase that stereotype. Among them is teaching our own children the difference between right and wrong. We've got to teach them skills so that they learn how to deal with disputes without resorting to violence. And we've got to teach them about responsibility and about the problems that having a baby out of wedlock can cause.

That's going to go a long way in repairing our image problem, brothas. And it's going to improve the quality of life for African-Americans across the country.

It's high time we got started on dealing with this. *(Feb. 19, 2002)*

FIRST BLACKS TO SERVE AS SAILORS FOUGHT THE ENEMY — AND RACISM — IN WWII

The crew of the Mason.

Before Black History Month gets away from us, we probably shouldn't forget the history created by the USS Mason DE529.

Thomas Howard of Cool Valley will never forget.

Howard was aboard the Mason, an escort ship that made history as the first Navy ship to go into war with a black crew. The ship, whose officers were white, was big news when it was launched in Boston in 1944. "Everyone came out for the launch," Howard recalled recently. "The governor, the mayor, folks from Hollywood like Dorothy Dandridge and Ossie Davis — they were all there."

Before the Mason's launch, blacks in the Navy were given menial work — serving white officers, shining shoes or handling mess duties. But with some nudging from Eleanor Roosevelt, President Franklin D. Roosevelt issued an order allowing blacks to serve as sailors.

The crew of the Mason had more than its share of white skeptics. "People were saying that we were too stupid to operate a ship, that we didn't have the intelligence to do anything like that," said Howard, 76. "So I think we were even more determined to succeed."

Many whites called the Mason "Eleanor's folly."

Howard and other sailors who served aboard the ship found themselves fighting the enemy, racism and rough weather in the North Atlantic, all at the same time.

The black sailors often ran into trouble with their white counterparts when the ship would stop at various ports. "There was entertainment at the USO in Plymouth, England, but the white sailors didn't want us dancing with the English women and caused trouble about it," Howard said. "Everywhere we went, we were subject to ridicule by white American soldiers. At one point, at a place in Plymouth called the Savoy, we were dancing with the native ladies when a group of white soldiers came along and asked them, 'How can you possibly dance with these so-and-sos?'"

A fight broke out, Howard said. "Finally, the Marines came in and helped us out."

They also dealt with discrimination at various ports when they would attempt to order food. "We'd want a place to get a Coke and a hot dog," Howard said. "But we often found that white servicemen had approached them before we got there and told them not to serve us."

Howard said he was surprised by the attitudes. He conceded that his life had been somewhat insulated, growing up in East St. Louis. "I guess I was naive," he said. "I knew that in St. Louis, we didn't have to go to the back of the streetcar or anything like that. At that time, I didn't know about the segregated toilets and segregated water fountains in St. Louis. I found out about that later."

In October 1944, the Mason had been at sea a month, guiding an unusual convoy of tugs and barges at very slow speeds across the ocean to Europe, when the weather turned bad. Barges broke loose and became dangerously huge projectiles. About a dozen crew members were lost at sea.

Then, without warning, the ship's deck split open. Water poured into the engine room. The cold water froze as soon as it hit the deck. The crew braved wind velocities of up to 40 mph, and the seas were up to about 40 feet. At one point, the ship took a 70-degree roll that made some crew members wonder if they would come back up.

But the crew miraculously welded a temporary fix to the crack. Two hours later they managed to bring the ship safely into port in England, and after strengthening the weld and pumping out the engine room, went right back out to sea to help rescue 12 other ships.

The crew escorted six convoys across the perilous North Atlantic from the weeks leading up to the D-Day invasion until V-E Day in 1945. The crew also protected transport ships from Nazi submarines.

The Mason saved lives, and that made a difference in the perception of some whites. In 1944, reporter Ollie Stewart wrote in the Baltimore Afro-American from the Italian front: "I have seen colored and white who glared at each other before a bombing get quite chummy after death whistled by in big hunks of shrapnel."

Still, when World War II ended, whites who had served aboard escort ships were honored. But there were no honors for the black sailors.

That changed in 1994 — nearly 50 years later, when President Bill Clinton honored those sailors. "For decades, African-Americans were missing in our memories of World War II," Clinton told the men in a White House ceremony. "In helping to show the world what America was against, you helped to show America what America is for. You helped liberate us all from segregation."

Because of a mix-up in records here, Howard did not receive his honors at the White House. They were mailed to him afterward.

Last year, the Navy honored the Mason when it launched a 6,500-ton destroyer that bears the same name.

Howard is proud of the service that he and his fellow sailors performed. "We showed this country what we could do if we were only given a chance," he said.

About 35 of the original 160-man crew of the Mason are believed to be alive today, and St. Louis is fortunate to be able to count Thomas Howard among them.

What better way to celebrate Black History Month than with someone who was part of it? *(Feb. 17, 2002)*

OLDER FOLKS' STORIES ABOUT THE PAST CAN TEACH US SOMETHING

How many of us — even when we have the chance — decline to take advantage of the knowledge that older people have?

I know I'm guilty. I have relatives who are seniors with whom I've been promising to sit down and listen to their stories, to learn about their lives.

Every so often, though, an opportunity falls into your hands. I had such an opportunity Wednesday, and I grabbed it with gusto.

Some readers may know that I also host "St. Louis on the Air," a talk show on KWMU radio. On Wednesday, Margaret Bush Wilson was my guest. She's an attorney, the first female national chair of the NAACP and the state's second black lawyer. Also with me was Charles Oldham, an attorney and longtime civil rights activist here. He and his late wife, Marian Oldham, were pioneers in efforts to seek equal accommodations for African-Americans here. Rounding out the panel was Norman Seay, a longtime civil rights activist and a founder of the St. Louis Committee on Racial Equality in 1947.

For an hour I was mesmerized as the three recounted the city's racial history. While they noted that St. Louis had no laws requiring blacks to sit at the back of the bus, as was the case in the South, most institutions were segregated by custom. Those who dared to challenge those customs were often tossed into jail.

Seay recalled a time when blacks could ride only the outside of streetcars. Oldham remembered a case where a black man who had very fair skin was taken to City Hospital, a whites-only facility. When hospital officials realized the man was black, they refused to admit him and sent him to Homer G. Phillips Hospital, which was for black patients. He died en route.

Wilson vividly recalled the Shelley vs. Kramer case that was argued before the U.S. Supreme Court in 1948. That decision effectively overturned racially restrictive housing covenants in St. Louis, opening housing markets to blacks. Wilson's father, James T. Bush, was a real estate broker who had mobilized other black brokers to legally challenge restricted agreements that barred the owners of property from selling or renting to "people not wholly of the Caucasian race."

"I heard that being discussed at the dinner table for four years," Wilson said.

While some believe that the idea of people conducting sit-ins at lunch counters to protest cafeterias that refused to serve blacks began with some hungry students in North Carolina in 1960, the panel noted that that was far from the truth. In 1950, members of the Committee on Racial Equality conducted sit-ins at the cafeteria of the old Stix, Baer & Fuller department store downtown.

None of the cafeteria boycotts was covered by the mainstream newspapers. The *Post-Dispatch*, *Globe-Democrat* and *Star-Times* all had policies against covering the sit-ins.

All three civil rights pioneers noted that both blacks and whites were involved in the effort to desegregate St. Louis' institutions. Wilson and Seay are black; Oldham is white.

"CORE was very integrated — and that wasn't unusual," Seay said. "There were many, many whites who helped pave the way for integrating many of our institutions."

Finally, after years of protest, the city approved a public accommodations measure in the mid-1960s.

Although it's far from perfect today, St. Louis has come a long way from the days described by these civil rights pioneers. That's why I chuckle when I sometimes hear young blacks complaining that nothing ever changes here.

Young people are, by nature, impatient. That's a redeeming characteristic. But it's important to look at the overall picture, to talk to older people who have been through a great deal, who have seen so much.

As for St. Louis, understanding our past can help us better understand ourselves.

Older people are blessed with knowledge. Those of us who are younger should listen to them more often. *(Nov. 8, 2001)*

HOTEL CHAIN IS ACCUSED OF DISCRIMINATION: WHAT ELSE IS NEW?

"Discrimination is a hellhound that gnaws at Negroes in every waking moment of their lives to remind them that the lie of their inferiority is accepted as truth in the society dominating them."

The Rev. Dr. Martin Luther King Jr., 1967

Some may have been surprised last week when the U.S. Justice Department filed a civil rights suit against the Adam's Mark hotel chain, charging it with repeatedly discriminating against African-Americans.

Not Antoine Coffer.

Coffer, the owner of Afrocentric Books in the city's West End, had experienced discrimination at the hotel firsthand.

A few years ago, when Coffer worked for a local tax firm, he and several other employees stopped into AJ's — the hotel's nightclub — for a drink. Coffer's colleagues were white; he is black.

"I was waiting and waiting at the bar, and the bartender kept ignoring me, passing over me for everyone else," Coffer said. When Coffer called it to the bartender's attention, the bartender responded with a racial slur, adding, "Who do you think you are?"

Coffer said he was stunned. So, he said, were his white colleagues, who stood up for him and confronted the bartender.

Coffer's story could have been unique. But his is far from the only horror story told about the place. In a 1996 effort to make the hotel comply with the nation's civil rights laws, U.S. District Judge Carol Jackson issued a memorandum based on testimony that managers had been told to hire only older black men as doormen at AJ's because that cultivated the "Old South" image that hotel president and chief executive officer Fred S. Kummer wanted. According to testimony, employees were instructed not to hire black waitresses for AJ's and not to play black music. Brands of liquor preferred by blacks were removed, and blue-eyed blondes were hired as waitresses.

Indeed, a mere sampling of the hotel chain's record makes one cringe. Among its problems:

* In 1992, a national black lawyers group moved its banquet from the hotel to a local church to protest the way its members were being treated.

* In 1993, the U.S. Equal Employment Opportunity Commission sued HBE Corp., owner of the Adam's Mark chain, over allegations that the hotel fired a personnel director because he refused to dismiss a black employee.

* In 1994, two former Adam's Mark managers won more than $4.9 million in a race discrimination suit, although the award was later drastically reduced. One manager said HBE officials failed to promote him and fired him in 1991 because he is black. The other manager, who is white, said he got fired when he objected to the firing of the black manager.

* In 1996, Kummer signed an agreement to ensure equal

employment opportunities after Denver Mayor Wellington Webb insisted he sign, or lose a $25 million city grant to help expand the Adam's Mark there.

* Earlier this year, the city of Clayton turned down HBE's proposal to build a new hotel complex after questioning the chain's record of racial and sexual harassment charges.

The list of shame goes on and on.

It's no surprise that a large corporation occasionally gets charged with discrimination, racial, sexual or otherwise. But when such allegations are made over and over again, year after year, it makes you wonder how big a fire is blazing beneath all the smoke. At the Adam's Mark, there seems to be a roaring inferno.

The most recent charges, filed by the Justice Department and the Florida attorney general's office, accuse the hotel chain of charging black customers higher prices than whites and segregating them in less desirable rooms as part of a corporate pattern of discrimination.

The new charges stem from allegations of discrimination by the hotel chain at its Daytona Beach property during an event in April known as Black College Weekend. The legal action contends that the hotel subjected black customers to stricter security, reservation and identification requirements. Black guests, but not white guests, were also made to wear orange wristbands to get into the hotel, the suit says.

That would have been plenty right there but, as the TV pitchmen say, "Wait, there's more." According to the suit, the 1,200 Black College Reunion guests were subjected to the removal of furniture such as couches, chairs and lamps from the lobby of the hotel on the day the Black College Reunion guests were to arrive; a removal of room amenities such as pictures and the failure to provide adequate housekeeping services, and a requirement that Black College Reunion guests pay cash for room service food and purchases at the hotel's restaurants and bars. The experience was both demeaning and humiliating.

During a news conference with U.S. Attorney General Janet Reno, Florida Attorney General Bob Butterworth called the hotel's behavior "disgraceful."

"Black patrons of the Adam's Mark resort were singled out and treated like second-class citizens," Butterworth said.

Reno agreed. In announcing the suit, she said, "It is hard to believe that 35 years after the Civil Rights Act was passed by Congress, this type of discrimination still exists."

Kummer continues to insist that it doesn't. He says that his company will be exonerated in the end. He even goes as far as to say that HBE has contributed to the United Negro College Fund.

Wow.

Meanwhile, Coffer, of Afrocentric Books, refuses to use the hotel anymore, as have many other black organizations. He is critical of black businesses that continue to use the hotel for dinner functions. He pointed to recent events there, such as the Missouri Black Expo and the St. Louis Sentinel dinner.

"Anyone who cares about how people are treated should boycott the Adam's Mark, in my opinion, and especially black businesses," Coffer said. "Seems to me that when we go there, we're buying into our own defeat. I mean, how do you sue your wife when you sleep with her every night?"

The federal case will eventually wind up in the courts, where a decision will be made as to whether the Adam's Mark is guilty of a pattern of discrimination against black guests and employees. Kummer and his company will have the chance to make their case in court. If the Justice Department and Florida attorney general cannot prove their case, then

Kummer has nothing to worry about.

But if the case is proved, and the Adam's Mark is found guilty, it should be penalized to the fullest extent of the law. After all, the hotel chain has had plenty of time to take care of its problems.

Enough is enough. *(Dec. 21, 1999)*

LACK OF BALANCE IS REAL MENACE

True confession time.

When I was a youngster, I enjoyed watching reruns of "Amos 'n' Andy."

Although I knew no one like Amos, Andy or their scheming comrade, the Kingfish, I would often sit in front of the big, boxy TV set that we had in those days and watch the show on Channel 11. I'd often smile, chuckle or outright guffaw at some of the things the characters said and did.

And then, one day, it wasn't on anymore. I didn't know it at the time, but the National Association for the Advancement of Colored People had forced the show to be yanked off the air and bought the rights to the show to keep it from airing again.

As I got older, I recognized the show's stereotyping, and for a long time I refused to tell anyone I had ever seen it.

I didn't understand why the NAACP did what it did then, but I understand now.

The problem with "Amos 'n' Andy" was not just that it was stereotypical. It was also the only television show featuring black people.

There was no balance. The Kingfish and his pals were buffoons.

Now, buffoons aren't new to television, and they come in all colors, sizes and shapes. From Ralph Kramden to Al Bundy, the time path of television is littered with buffoons.

But the difference between Ralph Kramden and the King-fish was that plenty of characters existed to balance off ol' Ralphie-boy. For every Ralph Kramden on television, there was a Dr. Kildare, a Roy Rogers, a Superman, an Eliot Ness.

But there was only "Amos 'n' Andy." That show produced the only consistent images of blacks on TV in those days. It provided the only exposure that many non-blacks had to blacks.

I thought about that last week as I listened to a talk by Robert Townsend. Townsend, the comedian who starred in such films as "Hollywood Shuffle" and "The Five Heartbeats," addressed the annual convention of the National Association of Black Journalists in Houston.

Townsend recalled that he had been in France a couple of years ago when a journalist called out to him as he headed to his car.

"Mr. Townsend, Mr. Townsend, what do you think of the status of the nigger in America?" the French journalist yelled.

Townsend said he turned around, addressed the journalist and said: "Hey, you should never, ever use that word."

"And then," Townsend said, "he said to me, 'But in American films that word is used all the time, especially by the black characters, and no one ever complains.'"

Townsend said the incident made him much more aware of the images of blacks that are projected.

"Amos 'n' Andy" was taken off the air because of the images of blacks — without balance — that were projected. The French journalist used the word because of the images of African-Americans — again without balance — that were projected, many by black filmmakers.

A line of black filmmakers has emerged in the 1990s, film-makers who are making films about black life in America. Some of the films have been powerful, many have been well-received by audiences. But for every film like "To Sleep With Anger," the powerful 1990 movie by Charles Burnett that dealt with issues of family and love, there are five like "Menace II Society." That's this year's film by Albert and Allen Hughes that features plenty of violence, drive-by shootings, drug abuse and foul language.

I don't object to the production of some of these violent films. They reflect a certain aspect of African-American life. But they hardly reflect a complete picture.

Problem is, people here and around the world think that these films reflect the essence of black life.

Hardly. Where is the joy, the love of children, the closeness of family, the sense of dignity that I see in African-American families every day? Why do I rarely see these families reflected on the big screen?

I felt a sense of pride a couple of years ago when black filmmakers arrived on the scene. At last, I thought, we will begin to see films that truly reflect the total African-American experience. Finally, blacks will be able to star in films that aren't comedies and have roles where they can portray detectives, police officers and strong heads of households.

At last, I thought, Hollywood will stop glorifying black movies like "Superfly," a drug pusher who became a role model to some youngsters.

With only a few exceptions, however, I've been disappointed. I've yet to see the diversity I'd hoped for.

But many of the new filmmakers, while talented, are young. Perhaps as they mature they will begin to broaden their scope.

Until they do, many of their films may do as much harm in the 1990s as "Amos 'n' Andy" did in the 1950s. (*July 27, 1993*)

RODNEY KING WOULD HATE RIOTS

When the verdict came down a year ago acquitting the four police officers who had been charged in the beating of Rodney King, I wrote that I understood the reactions of those who rioted because they were outraged at what had happened.

Many people — especially Los Angeles' poor — had put their faith in the justice system. They, as we, had all seen King on videotape beaten beyond belief. There could be no verdict other than guilty, many had assumed. The system will work and justice will be meted out properly.

But when it didn't work out that way, many people were outraged and expressed their frustration in any way that they could.

I understood the frustrations — I was frustrated as well — but couldn't agree with their reactions. Burning down your community is no way to vent your anger. Many people in south-central Los Angeles — who are today out millions of dollars and countless jobs — surely realize that as well.

That's why it's good that efforts are being made here and across the country to prevent a violent reaction to the verdict of the federal case that's going through the courts now. A verdict will come down any day, and a great deal of preparation is being made to try to blunt any violent reaction.

On Sunday, as they were discussing the importance of Easter, a good many ministers were also talking about the dangers of rioting. Many pointed out, rightly, that the losers in riots are generally the ones who do the rioting. Riots are rarely organized. They often occur on the spot. The homes of the rioters are the ones that are destroyed. Their businesses are the ones burned to the ground. Their neighborhood markets are the ones wiped out. They are the ones who will have to walk 12 blocks to shop rather than go to the store in their neighborhood.

In short, they are the ones who are hurt most by any riot. The same is the case here.

As anywhere, there will always be people who enjoy nothing more than to start trouble wherever they go. And, sure enough, some here are circulating fliers suggesting that when the verdict comes down, people should go to specific locations to riot.

Nothing could be more foolish.

No matter what happens here, it will have no effect on the Rodney King case. That case is in Los Angeles. To burn down a house here, or a block of houses or a whole neighborhood, will do absolutely nothing for Rodney King or for justice or for the people of south-central LA.

What it will do will be to make life harder for some people who are trying to make it just like anyone else.

Like many who have watched that videotape over and over, there is no question in my mind as to the guilt of the police officers. But I'm not on the jury. Those people who are on the jury — and who have listened to a string of witnesses telling them that they didn't see what they think they saw — are the ones who have to make the final decision. This time, we can hope, justice will be served.

After the riots in Los Angeles last year, we saw a rainbow of volunteers work hard to clean up the wreckage and put that community back again. In fact, the rioters, the victims and the volunteers were from all walks of life and from all ethnic groups. Many of them invested not only time but hope, hope in the idea that what had happened would not happen again.

In the aftermath of last year's events — including the incident with Reginald Denny, the white motorist who was yanked from his truck and beaten mercilessly by a group of black thugs — there are plenty of people ready and willing to take advantage of it all.

There were those who did so last year. Firebrands like Al Sharpton and rappers Chuck D. and KRS-One, who expressed their anger at whites for taking advantage of blacks. Firebrands like then-presidential candidate Patrick Buchanan, who expressed his anger at blacks for taking advantage of whites.

There are those who are drooling for the chance to do so again.

Rodney King uttered perhaps the wisest words of all last year when he asked, "Can we get along?"

Can we get along? Can we learn to treat people decently? Can we at least try?

No one knows what the verdict will be in the federal case. But whatever the verdict, let's hope that people, both here and in Los Angeles, react using two very basic things — common sense and human decency. *(April 13, 1993)*

BLACK HISTORY DESERVES MORE THAN A MONTH

I'm eagerly awaiting the day when there is no longer a Black History Month.

That's right. I'd like to see the special celebration done away with. That's because I'm looking forward to a time when we no longer need a special month to study black history.

The whole idea of Black History Month — which actually began as Negro History Week — was developed in 1926 by historian Carter G. Woodson. He developed the concept and promoted the week because at that time, black contributions had been all but ignored by schools of lower and higher education. To change that, Woodson established Negro History Week.

Incidentally, for those conspiracy theorists out there who think that February was chosen because it is the shortest month in the year, think again. Woodson chose February because it contained the birthdates of both Abraham Lincoln and Frederick Douglass.

Woodson's notion was initially laughed at by whites. How could there possibly be enough contributions by blacks to fill up an entire week? The whole idea was ridiculous, some suggested. But Woodson persisted, and Negro History Week eventually became Black History Month because of the many contributions by blacks in America and around the world.

A few things have changed since 1926. Black history courses have sprung up in schools throughout the country. And Black History Month is observed in many areas each February.

So what's the problem now?

While much time and effort is spent during the month of February recognizing the achievements of blacks, those achievements are virtually invisible during the other 11 months of the year. Rather than being included in regular American and world history courses, black history is set apart as being something different.

Surely we can do better than that.

Each February, I can always count on numerous requests from schools and other organizations for me to come and speak about black history. I'm not alone in this. Many of my journalistic colleagues, both at the *Post-Dispatch* and at other news organizations, receive similar requests.

But some of my colleagues have decided to say no to Black History Month requests.

"One month out of the year," one colleague told me. "I'm only asked to speak about black history one month out of the year. I've decided to say no to any requests during February. I'll be glad to talk about black history the other 11 months."

The whole issue of history is a touchy one. There are college professors who actually believe that including blacks in courses on world history would somehow bastardize the teaching of history. They believe that by including blacks in their teaching they would somehow be bowing to the world of political correctness.

I suggest that, instead, it might be a bow to the world of accuracy.

The contributions of blacks to the world's development have been ignored for centuries and are only now finding their way into history books. The same can be said of Native Americans who, until only recently, were portrayed in many history books as little more than savages who had to be tamed.

The past, the present and the future are inevitably linked. How does one look toward one's future without being able to look at one's past? How can people learn from their mistakes if they don't realize them? How can a clear and accurate portrait of America be painted without all of the elements that make the subject so special?

The history of blacks is especially important for youngsters. For black youngsters, it's important for self-esteem. Obstacles seem less daunting when young people realize that others have jumped over similar hurdles. For non-black youngsters, the knowledge is equally important. They may be unaware of the contributions that blacks have made to this nation and to the world.

Many blacks and whites may be unaware that a black, Benjamin Banneker, built the first wooden clock in the United States and later was a surveyor on a six-man team that helped lay out Washington, D.C., for example. They may not know that another black, Garrett Morgan, invented the first traffic light. They may never have heard of Daisy Bates, a newspaper publisher in Little Rock, Ark., who helped champion the integration of Central High School in the 1950s.

Without knowledge of the contributions that blacks have made here and elsewhere, youngsters are, in effect, being culturally deprived.

I hope that one day within my lifetime we'll see a time when Black History Month becomes history itself. That's when we'll know that something significant has been accomplished in America. *(Feb. 23, 1993)*

I SAY KEEP SEN. LOTT ON — AS A CONSTANT REMINDER TO US ALL

Don't count me among those calling for Sen. Trent Lott to step down.

To the contrary, I'm one who thinks Lott should retain both his Senate seat and his leadership position in Congress.

Lott has taken a lot of heat recently because of his remarks at Sen. Strom Thurmond's 100th birthday party this month. At that party, Lott said that the nation would have been better off had Thurmond, who ran for president on a segregationist platform in 1948, been elected. In Lott's own words: "I want to say this about my state (Mississippi): When Strom Thurmond ran for president, we voted for him. We're proud of it. And if the rest of the country had followed our lead, we wouldn't have had all these problems over all these years, either."

Lott has been drawing heat for those remarks since he made them Dec. 5, although he has apologized for them several times. Still, people from all sides are calling for him to step down, at least as a leader of the Republican Party.

I wish they'd back off.

If you've ever taken a close look at Trent Lott, there's never been a real question about where he stood on issues of race. In fact, during a political rally in 1980, Lott had this to say, again referring to Thurmond: "You know, if we had elected this man 30 years ago, we wouldn't be in the mess we are today."

It's clear where Lott stands. He feels we would be better off if we were back in the days of separate water fountains, schools and lives. His supposed slip of the tongue is backed up by his record, including his votes against civil rights legislation, his votes against the Martin Luther King holiday and his push for anti-busing legislation.

And while some are shocked by what he said most recently, we're putting our heads in the sand if we want to believe that what he's saying isn't believed by others.

Is it believed by a majority of whites? I hardly think so. But it's apparently believed by a large enough percentage to get him re-elected to the Senate every six years and to propel him to the top leadership of his party.

Apparently, those folks haven't considered his remarks so outrageous as to not support him.

Some African-Americans are among the most vocal in calling for Lott to resign. Tom Joyner, who hosts the nation's largest black-audience radio show, told the "Today" show on Monday that Lott couldn't apologize enough and that he should go. And as much as I like Joyner, I've got to disagree with him.

Think about the advantages of having Lott remain. It could only be a positive step for African-Americans. With Lott as a key spokesman for his party, the GOP would be hamstrung when it comes to passing any legislation that would remotely appear regressive to black Americans.

There are other advantages to keeping Lott in office. At a time when some would have Americans believe that racism has now miraculously vanished from America's landscape, Trent Lott is there, a reminder that while some of the battles have been successfully fought, the war isn't over yet.

Let's be honest: Racism in this country has diminished considerably since Strom Thurmond's Dixiecrat days of the late 1940s. Much of that has been because of civil rights activists, both black and white, who strongly pushed against a segregated America.

In today's politically correct world, it's improper to say hateful things in public, even if they are what you're really thinking.

But Lott said what he thought. And I think we should keep him as a top leader in the Senate.

There, he can continue to serve as a symbol, a reminder that just because fewer people publicly make racist comments these days, it doesn't mean the problem has gone away. It's simply gone underground. *(Dec. 17, 2002)*

BLACKS, JEWS TEAM UP, GIVE PUPILS A BOOST

Experts may fret over the state of black-Jewish relations in America, but not so members of the Cote Brilliante Presbyterian Church and the Central Reform Congregation.

The two groups have developed a close working relationship that has resulted in a mentoring program at one of the city's public schools.

Since October, 87 members of Cote Brilliante, at 4673 Labadie Avenue, and Central Reform, at 77 Maryland Plaza, have met once a month with 87 first-grade students at Cote Brilliante School, 2616 Cora Avenue. On those days, they have worked one-on-one with the students from 8:30 a.m. to 9:30 a.m.

Ivory Johnson, who's coordinating the efforts at Cote Brilliante Church, said the mentors hope to motivate the youngsters, especially in attendance. The mentors hope to work with the students through elementary school.

"We know that most mentoring programs are done with

students who are in higher grades," Johnson said. "But the principal thought that the program would be more beneficial if we worked with the kids from the first grade and stuck with them throughout elementary school.

"We're not teachers, so we're not really tutoring or anything like that. What we want to focus on is motivation and self-esteem, and make the kids feel good about themselves. We also want to let them know that someone cares about them beside their teachers and their parents."

The mentors, with the help of the city schools' drug-free program, have developed activities for the children. For example, Central Reform volunteers made pencil holders covered with stamps from around the world for each of the youngsters. And Cote Brilliante Church volunteers made bookcases for each child out of cardboard boxes.

"The idea behind these is to motivate," Johnson said. "If there's a pencil holder, hopefully the child will get pencils. If there's a bookcase, hopefully the child will get books."

Chris Hexter, who coordinates the efforts of Central Reform, said the mentors have collected books and have been able to give each child a book each time the mentors and students have met. "We hope that helps to motivate the youngsters to read," he said.

The volunteers haven't left out the parents of the first graders.

"We met with the students and their parents and guardians on a Saturday afternoon in November, and we've tried to have activities to involve the whole family," Hexter said. For example, families and mentors attended a play in March on Harriet Tubman at the Center of Contemporary Arts.

The mentors don't want to stop there, however.

They are planning to continue their efforts with the youngsters over the summer at Cote Brilliante church.

One of the sessions being planned features Washington University professor Gerald Early, who will discuss good writing. The mentors also hope to put together a program with the St. Louis Symphony.

"We've also been able to bring some resources to the school," Johnson said. "For example, we've been able to provide calculators for all of the fifth-graders, mittens for all the kids in the school and turkeys for the family of every first-grader."

"We'd like to be able to provide some resources for other grades as well," Hexter said. He noted that the two religious institutions are planning a health fair for the fall.

Both men said that it had taken some effort to put the program together. "It's not the easiest thing in the world to get 87 people — 50 percent from each congregation — to volunteer to be mentors," Hexter said. Both men said they were fortunate to have the support of Rabbi Susan Talve of Central Reform and the Rev. William Gillespie at Cote Brilliante.

Some mentors had become so gung-ho that they had begun to visit the students at home and to give gifts to the youngsters.

"We had a little problem there," Johnson said. "We didn't want some kids getting gifts and other kids getting none. And we didn't want kids to be disappointed when a mentor showed up without a gift. So, we've decided that if we give a gift to one kid, we've got to give gifts to them all."

"But we decided that a gift of time is OK," Hexter added.

The mentoring program has helped cement a relationship between the two religious institutions that was begun in 1991 and which now includes an annual program at Cote Brilliante Church celebrating the birthday of the Rev. Dr. Martin Luther King Jr., and invitations for all to participate in the Jewish holidays of Rosh Hashana and Yom Kippur. Congregants recently attended the play "Jar the Floor" at the Black Rep and plan a meeting with Police Chief Clarence Harmon as the speaker.

"We're committed to working together as long as there's interest," Hexter said. "I think we all want to do what we can to help the community." *(May 16, 1993)*

Part 4:

Love,
Hope,
Survival

HOW DO YOU GO ABOUT ASKING SOMEONE TO DONATE A KIDNEY?

In July last year, I was hit with a double whammy.

Within 10 days, I was told that I was suffering from muscular dystrophy and that my kidneys were failing.

Worse yet, doctors weren't sure of the cause of either ailment, and they saw no connection between the two.

For the muscular dystrophy — limb girdle muscular dystrophy, to be exact — there is no cure, no medicines to take. I would find my muscles gradually weakening.

For the kidneys, my options were few: They boiled down to eventually going on dialysis for the rest of my life, or getting a kidney transplant.

So later this week — about 16 months after learning about my kidneys — I'll undergo a kidney transplant. That means I won't be writing for a while. My recovery should take several weeks, and I expect to resume this column in January.

When I learned that I was afflicted with both ailments, I was in shock and considerably depressed. I decided I wouldn't tell anyone about either until it was necessary. I didn't want people feeling sorry for me. While people have died of kidney failure, I didn't want people looking at me as if I was going to die. Besides, I felt fine, even though things were going on inside of me.

Eventually, my walking became more difficult. Even though I had started using a cane to get around, I joked with my wife that I still walked like a very slow Herman Munster.

But I had to learn more about my kidneys. At a seminar I attended, speakers who had dealt with failing kidneys spoke about their experiences. I left the seminar with more hope than I had had before. I concluded that I would try to get a kidney transplant.

But that, it turned out, was easier said than done. There is a waiting list for cadaver kidneys. Although it costs nothing to donate your organs for use after you die, not nearly enough people do so. About 75,000 people are on the waiting list.

But over the years, I had interviewed people who had gone through dialysis, and I knew how difficult it was for some of them. Some hadn't tolerated the dialysis well at all. And many people have to go for dialysis for four hours a day, three times a week.

To qualify as a potential kidney recipient, I had to go through a battery of tests that seemed to go on forever. But I qualified. Then I figured that all I'd have to do was sit back and wait for the call.

But as I waited — and waited — my kidney function diminished. At one point, my doctor told me that my kidneys were functioning at 11 percent of normal. I began feeling weak and tired. I began receiving once-a-week injections of a drug to fight anemia, but it was only a temporary fix. The kidneys were failing faster than I was moving up on the donor list. I had to find a live kidney donor or face dialysis. And it couldn't be just anyone; it had to be someone with Type O blood.

I gave it a lot of thought. How do you ask someone for a kidney? Finally, I ended up writing letters to several friends and relatives, explaining to them what was happening with me and asking if they would consider donating. I felt awkward asking; I knew the letter would make some people feel uncomfortable, especially if they felt they had to say no. I explained in the letter that I would understand if they turned me down because it was such a personal request.

People responded differently, and some chose not to respond at all. But two friends agreed to be tested to see if they were a match. My sister also agreed to be tested. And it turned out she was a match. Although she was nervous about the idea of surgery, she agreed to do it.

Needless to say, my sister, Cheryl McKinney, is my heroine. What greater love can there be between a brother and a sister than when one agrees to give an organ to another? I can never express how grateful I am to her, how blessed I am to have her as a sister.

So this week, I'll undergo surgery. It's one surgery that I'm actually looking forward to.

The next few weeks won't be easy ones for me. But they will be worth it.

I'm sure of that. *(Nov. 27, 2001)*

I HAD TWO KIDNEYS, AND NOW I'VE GOT THREE: LET'S GO TO WORK

So, where were we?

That seems to be the appropriate question to ask after being gone from the pages of the newspaper for six weeks.

I underwent kidney transplant surgery at the end of November. I was fortunate in that my sister, Cheryl McKinney, agreed to donate a kidney to me.

As a bit of background, I learned in 2000 that my kidneys were failing and that I would ultimately have to go on dialysis or get a transplant. The idea of dialysis wasn't appealing, especially because I had interviewed people in the past who had told me how grueling dialysis was for them. I got on the waiting list for a kidney.

Over time, however, my kidneys worsened, and I began asking friends and relatives if they might be willing to donate. Along came my sister to the rescue.

Surgery is an interesting process. The morning of the surgery, the patients are put in a room similar to the way airplanes are put in a holding pattern on the runway as they await an all-clear from the control tower. Cheryl and I were next to one another, and she went in first. As she headed in for her surgery, she gave me a thumbs-up sign. I gave her one back.

About a half-hour later, I was called in for surgery. I remember arriving at the operating room. The next thing I remember, it was evening and I was being wheeled to my room, surgery completed.

The surgery was successful, thanks to our surgeons, Dr. Jeffrey Lowell and Dr. Surendra Shenoy, and thanks to the good care we received from the doctors, nurses and staff at Barnes-Jewish Hospital. Neither my sister nor I are back to full strength, but we're getting there, slowly but surely.

For me, the surgery itself wasn't terribly painful. In fact, having a catheter removed was probably the most painful ordeal that I went through.

I now have three kidneys, two that virtually shut down following the surgery, and the new one, which is working as it should. I feel good, my appetite's fine, and so far I've received a clean bill of health.

In my last column, I mentioned that I also suffer from something called limb girdle muscular dystrophy. As a result of the surgery, my muscles were weakened, and it took a couple of weeks before I could even walk. I'm still not back to the strength I was before the surgery, but I'm hoping it will return. If I've learned anything, it's that good health is a precious commodity.

Following the surgery, I was overwhelmed by the love and concern of friends, colleagues and readers of my column. Between letters, e-mails, cards, flowers and gift baskets, I easily heard from thousands of people, wishing me well, offering prayers and giving support. While I wasn't able to respond to each personally, I will forever be grateful to all of those I heard from. It meant a great deal to me.

A key to my recovery has been my family. From my wife and son, who were tremendously supportive, to my mother, who let me live with her for several weeks as I recovered, to my cousin, Reginald Dilworth, who spent weeks with me as a sort of personal-care attendant, my family was terrific through the entire ordeal.

I consider my sister's donation of her kidney to be a blessing. Unfortunately, there aren't nearly enough blessings around. I hope people will consider being organ donors. Sign the back of your license, and let family members know of your wishes. If you have the opportunity to be a living donor, give it serious thought. Thousands are waiting, and a donation can make the difference between whether someone lives or dies.

Meanwhile, what's next for me? Back to work. Journalism is a "What-have-you-done-for-me-lately?" business, so for me, it will be nose to the grindstone, three columns a week. And starting today, I'll be back on "St. Louis on the Air," the radio program that I host on KWMU-FM.

Let's roll. *(Jan. 15, 2002)*

A SISTER'S GIFT OF LOVE, HOPE & SURVIVAL

It's been two years now since I got the devastating news: My kidneys were failing and I should prepare for dialysis.

Dialysis meant I would have to spend four hours a day, three times a week, at a center where a machine would do the work my kidneys were increasingly incapable of performing — filter the toxins from my blood. Without dialysis, my doctor told me, I would die. With dialysis, my prospects would be merely grim. Forty percent of dialysis patients die in the first two years, and complications frequently arise, not the least of which is fatigue.

My career as a columnist and radio talk-show host is time-consuming and fulfilling. The prospect of spending so much time on dialysis seemed unbearable.

But then I was given some hope. If I could get a kidney transplant, I could avoid dialysis.

I went through all of the required screenings and work-ups and was found eligible to be put on the waiting list. I was given a pager, and told that when it went off, it would mean that a kidney was available.

At first, I was excited, listening intently to the pager, expecting it to go off at any minute. But the minutes turned to hours, the hours to days, the days to months. I never got a page.

Meanwhile, my kidney function declined. When I got home each evening, I was exhausted, falling asleep almost anywhere. With the help of my kidney specialist, Dr. David Windus, I was able to take weekly injections of Procrit, a drug that stimulates red blood cells, to keep me going.

Desperate, I began inquiring among a few relatives and friends, asking them, in effect: Brother, can you spare a kidney?

As it turned out, it was my sister, Cheryl McKinney, who came to my rescue by donating her kidney. Cheryl and I underwent surgery last November, and we're both doing fine. I am among 550 fortunate people in the St. Louis area who got organ transplants last year.

Sadly, though, everyone isn't so fortunate.

America faces a critical shortage of donated organs. As of this month, more than 79,000 Americans are on waiting lists for such organs as kidneys, liver, hearts and lungs, according to the United Network for Organ Sharing. That compares to only about 18,000 people in 1989. Between 1988 and last year, more than 21,500 Americans on waiting lists died, hoping for organ donations that never came.

The irony of the donor situation is that while doctors have become more proficient at transplants, the nation is suffering from a shortage of donated organs. As I learned during my own quest, many people are squeamish about the idea of donating organs — when they are living or after they've died.

Some would-be organ donors refuse to participate because they wonder if doctors will be too eager to harvest their organs if they ever end up on a hospital's critical list. Family members are often reluctant to donate the organs of loved ones because they are already distraught.

But the role of loved ones is vital. Many people are under the misconception that if they sign the back of their drivers license, their organs will be donated. In fact, those signatures have no legal effect. Under the law, only a donor's survivors can agree to donate a person's organs. For that reason, it's important for potential donors to make their loved ones aware of their wishes.

Even potential live donors often have reservations. My sister had plenty.

"I was nervous and somewhat afraid, and I wondered if I would be OK afterward," she said. "After all, I have a husband and three children, and I worried about what would happen to them if something happened to me."

And, of course, there is some risk. Cheryl underwent major surgery, and now she will spend the rest of her life without a backup in case her kidney fails.

Cheryl was one of several people I approached to see if they would be tested as a match for me. Knowing the request was awkward, I sent out several letters to relatives and friends asking them if they would consider it. I didn't get responses from everyone. I expected that. That's why I wrote the letters. If they weren't interested in the idea, they wouldn't have to feel uncomfortable telling me no; they simply could choose not to respond.

But Cheryl responded.

Cheryl is four years younger than I, and as kids, we fought like cats and dogs. I was more introverted and studious; she was more outgoing and fun-loving. She had a quick temper; I was more likely to keep things inside.

But as we've grown older, we've grown closer. We sometimes talk on the phone for hours.

In that sense, then, perhaps it was no surprise that Cheryl agreed to be tested. She thought she wouldn't be a match. She thought that she had remembered from years earlier that we had two different blood types. As it turns out, though, her memory was faulty. The introvert and the extrovert matched.

Cheryl still then had to make the decision. "I knew I had to do what I had to do," she said. "But I had so many questions. Would it change my life? Could I continue the way I was?"

After getting assurances — from doctors and from others who had gone through the procedure — Cheryl decided to do it.

We checked into the hospital the day before the surgery. The morning of the surgery, Cheryl came to my room, and we held hands and said a little prayer.

In no time, we were transported to a pre-operation room,

where we were lined up in order, much like airplanes on a runway. Lying on beds next to each other, we exchanged small talk.

"Are you nervous?" she asked.

"Yeah, I am," I told her. "Are you cold?"

"Yes, it is a little cold in here. I wonder if we can get some warm blankets."

Cheryl was rolled into surgery first. As she looked at me one last time, she gave me a thumbs-up sign. I gave one back to her.

It would be nearly 36 hours before we would see each other again. After my surgery, I was placed in an observation room for 24 hours, and Cheryl was unable to visit me. But after I was taken to a regular patient room, she came to visit. I was amazed. She looked great. She said she felt fine. And she had walked from her room to mine, something I didn't think she would be able to do right away.

Last week, I asked her if she felt any differently now than before the surgery.

"You know what? I feel exactly the same as I did before I donated the kidney," she said. "I don't feel any different. I'm able to do the same things that I could do before. In fact, sometimes I think that I could close my eyes and it would be as if it were all a dream. I haven't changed a bit. The only difference is that I now have a scar from the surgery."

Dr. Jeffrey Lowell believes there would be more organ donations if the medical industry and others would be more effective in educating the public. Lowell is a liver and kidney transplant surgeon at Barnes-Jewish Hospital and St. Louis Children's Hospital. He was also my surgeon.

"I'm afraid we've done a poor job of marketing," Lowell said. "In our society, we can sell all sorts of things for cash money but can't seem to come up with a way to effectively sell the idea of donating organs — which costs nothing."

Lowell compares that to recycling. "God forbid I should throw an aluminum can in the trash these days," he said. "I feel guilty. We've taught our society a lot about recycling and caring about the environment since the time that I was a kid. . . . Somehow, we've got to convince people that recycling organs is just as important. I mean, transplants work, and they help real people all the time. But I'm not so sure the general public knows that."

I'm one who knows that transplants work. I also know that had I not received an organ donation, I could have died. Dialysis works for only so long. And while a donated organ doesn't mean that a person never has to worry again — after all, I have to take a variety of pills each day to suppress my immune system so that my body doesn't reject my new kidney — it can improve a person's quality of life tremendously.

I can say one thing with certainty: Whenever I die, I plan to donate my organs to those who can use them.

Let my loved ones take notice. *(April 21, 2002)*

THE INCREDIBLE SHRINKING MAN

A year ago at this time, I was huge.

Not huge in the sense of being famous or popular.

No, I mean, I was immense.

Immense probably isn't the word. Try the Goodyear blimp. Think about Dumbo, the baby elephant (OK, my ears are smaller). Children thought I was a float in the Macy's parade.

I wasn't always so big. Although small has never been an appropriate adjective to describe me, I had been better about watching my weight. But in recent years, I'd watched it go up and up and up. Weight control has never been one of my strong points. I like food too much. There was a time when anything that even looked similar to a powdered doughnut never stood a chance with me.

But last year, I decided to do something about it. I increased my exercise, joined Weight Watchers and lost 72 pounds. I'm still working at it and hope to lose a lot more. I don't look like Denzel Washington (I'm afraid it would take a lot more than weight loss for me to do that), but I no longer resemble a beach ball with legs.

It hasn't been easy. It's taken some work and discipline.

I know some thin folks who think it's no problem to lose weight. Just do it, they say.

I've learned from experience that it takes a little more than that. It may be easier for them because they don't weigh nearly as much. For me, it's taken some effort.

But, and I'm glad to say this, it really hasn't meant depriving myself of the foods I like.

It has meant going about this whole eating thing a little differently and with a little moderation. The old seafood diet joke — I see food and I eat it — certainly applied to me before last year. Anything I saw and liked, I ate. I didn't pay attention to the fat content, sodium content or anything else.

I've begun paying more attention these days, and I'm trying better to eat three meals a day instead of eating one or two big meals a day and snacking the rest of the time.

Breakfast for me used to consist of a Belgian waffle smothered in butter, several link sausages, scrambled eggs and buttered toast. That probably made me a lead contender for the Mr. Cholesterol award, not to mention a good prospect for a heart attack.

Today, breakfast is more likely to consist of a bagel and a cup of decaf coffee. The amazing thing is that it satisfies me just as much.

What about the old stuff I used to eat? Do I still have a desire for it?

Sometimes, and occasionally, I'll even get it. I had an urge a few months ago for some chicken from London and Sons Wing House. I got an order of juicy chicken wings covered with ketchup and hot sauce, and a side of fries. If you haven't had them, I'll vouch for how good they are. But I'll also tell you they're probably not on any cardiologist's proposed diet.

I wanted them, I got them and the urge was gone. And then I ate better the next day.

I've learned that losing weight doesn't have to mean that you stop eating what you like. It simply means that you eat better — more vegetables, less fat and with moderation.

And for me it's also meant walking, something that I really enjoy. It's a lot of fun to take in the scenery around me. We take so much for granted as we drive around. Walking through Forest Park or down the streets of my neighborhood, I find there's so much that I never really knew existed. I can enjoy the serenity of an early morning, listen to the birds making music overhead, admire the architecture of fine old buildings.

All that, and I'm doing something healthy at the same time.

Many people have always known that these things are a way to lose weight or keep it under control. But for some of us, the lesson's come late.

I've learned that by doing things like paying attention to what you eat, being aware of what foods amount to empty calories, reading the scale regularly and upping the exercise, you don't have to be the Goodyear blimp if you really don't want to. So I'll continue this regimen and, with any success, continue losing weight.

Don, who heads my particular Weight Watchers group, tells us at the end of each session: "I hope to see a little less of you next week."

By this time next year, I hope you'll see a little less of me. *(Feb. 27, 1996)*

MEN CAN LEARN FROM WOMEN TO BETTER CARE FOR THEMSELVES

During my recent bout with prostate cancer, I've begun to learn the difference between men and women.

Some of those differences I knew already, of course. My wife has been the great teacher in this effort.

She and I share a mutual friend who's been divorced twice and who is constantly dating, ever hoping to meet wife No. 3. He and I get together for dinner or drinks every so often.

Without a doubt, when I return home, my wife asks me who he's dating or how his wife hunt is going. And almost every time I turn to her and tell her I don't know. She stares at me incredulously.

See, that's one of the differences between men and women. Women are much more personal than men. I wouldn't think of prying into my friend's love life to find out who he's dating or whether he's found any good prospects. My way of thinking is that that's private information. If my friend decides he wants to talk to me about it, fine. If not, I won't ask him. To do so would be to break the unspoken code of men.

But had my friend been a woman and had gone out with my wife, I'm sure my wife would have returned with how many men the friend had been dating, what their names were, where they worked and what their Social Security numbers were.

Forget everything else. What I've described is the basic difference between men and women.

That difference became abundantly clear within the last month as I wrote about my prostate cancer surgery.

I heard from quite a few men who had had similar surgery, with all sorts of good advice. But for many of them, it was as if I was on the streets of New York while someone in a raincoat whispered to me, "Pssst. Want to buy a watch?"

I got the sense that for many of these guys, prostate cancer surgery was something to keep quiet about, something to never talk about. That wasn't the case with everyone, of course, but it seemed to be that way for many.

And it began to make clear that difference between men and women: Women are more willing to share their personal experiences. And it's made a difference for them.

Take a look at breast cancer. It's been at least 20 years since women began openly discussing that issue. Now you see the issue all over television. Mothers teach their daughters how to check for it. Television announcers urge women to get checked for it. Because women are much more open with this kind of stuff, they're educating one another much more than men are.

Rarely have I seen any public service announcements about prostate cancer. Not once has any older man in my family encouraged me to be tested annually for prostate cancer. This is something we just don't — or can't — talk about much.

I asked my surgeon, Dr. William Catalona, about it. "I think that's really true, that women are much more open to discussions of this sort than men," said Catalona, a prostate cancer specialist at Barnes-Jewish Hospital. "Perhaps it's because that with the childbearing experience, women get used to seeing OB/Gyns and being examined. They're more used to breast and pelvic examinations."

Perhaps that's it. There's something about men being more uncomfortable with talking about personal issues than women. It's why, in our culture, it's OK for women to cry but it's less OK for men to do so. We're supposed to be stronger. Be better. Less interested in personal things.

In fact, though, we can learn from women. We need to pay closer attention to ourselves. While I'm still not willing to ask my friend about his love life when I see him, I'm more willing today to encourage him to be examined for prostate cancer and to have a PSA blood test done. It's a bit more personal than what I would have said to him, say, a year ago.

But I've learned that sometimes being personal can save lives.

For those who have asked, my surgery went well. My cancer did not spread. It was limited to my prostate gland, and there was no trace of the disease in my lymph nodes. Thanks to so many of you for your prayers, your calls, e-mail, letters, visits and flowers during my recent surgery. I was overwhelmed by your goodwill.

While I'm giving praise, thanks to Dr. Catalona and his staff, the medical and nursing staff at Barnes-Jewish Hospital, and the other doctors and nurses who helped me in my recent bout. I'm still recuperating from the surgery, but plan to be back at work shortly, good as new. Thanks for all of your support. *(April 11, 1999)*

SIGHTS, SOUNDS AND TASTES OF HOSPITAL MADE COLUMNIST READY TO COME HOME

An unexpected emergency.

It wasn't supposed to happen this way.

I'd pulled a muscle earlier in the week, and the pain had remained with me. I'd planned a visit to the doctor. He would fix me up with some pills or a quick shot, or so I thought.

I'd planned a busy day. Lunch with one fellow, a couple of interviews, a column to write.

My doctor had other plans.

He looked at me and told me I had a hernia.

OK, I thought. I'd better get the prescription for something to take care of that and then move on. It's not going to be that simple, the doctor told me. I had an "incarcerated hernia," he told me, and it was likely that surgery would be the only way to repair it.

Wow. More serious than I'd thought. OK, I figured, I'd better check my schedule and see when I might be able to go in for surgery.

Again, my doctor had other ideas.

"I think you may have to have surgery right away," he told me.

From that moment on, my life was a whirlwind. No time to go home to pack. No time to plan for this. Just a straight drive to the hospital.

On the way over I hopped on the phone, canceled my lunch, my interviews and called my bosses to tell them what was happening.

Once I got to the hospital, I was interviewed by a bevy of doctors who asked me the same questions over and over.

Why was I there? Did I feel pain? Did it hurt when they did this? (It did.)

Next came the vampire factor. A nurse came in and took several tubes of blood from me, convincing me that a career counselor would have advised Count Dracula to work in a hospital.

An IV was put into my arm, I was wheeled into another room, where I met my anesthesiologist. This is a person who you see for a couple of minutes and then forget everything.

The anesthesiologist put something in my IV, I looked over at my wife and whispered "I love you," and that was all I remembered.

The next thing I knew, I was waking up, lying in a hospital bed, my wife waiting for me. She asked how I felt.

"Mmmmmmf," I mumbled. It took a few minutes for my

mouth to catch up with my mind so that I could actually speak words. Once I could speak, my throat was sore. I was in a narrow bed with railings on both sides.

My wife kissed me and told me she'd see me the next day.

Nighttime in a hospital is anything but a stay at the Comfort Inn, and I had a hard time sleeping.

Because of my surgery, I couldn't really toss and turn in bed. I felt restricted. I was cold. The IV machine kept beeping. I'd doze off and be awakened because I was cold. A nurse brought me some warm blankets. But I still couldn't sleep. I asked for something to help me sleep, and a nurse brought me a couple of tablets to take. I took them and finally dropped off, only to be awakened 10 minutes later. "Time to check your vitals," a cheery nurse said, thermometer in one hand, blood pressure cuff in the other.

I was reminded of an old Three Stooges routine, where Moe slaps a sleeping Larry and says, "Hey numbskull, wake up and go to sleep." I kept looking for Curley to show up.

Meal times in the hospital were another matter. Nurses expressed a concern that I never ate everything in the meal.

It wasn't because I was sick; it was because, well, let's just say hospital food leaves a lot to be desired. I found myself asking questions like how can turkey smothered in gravy be dry? Is there anything more bland than hospital noodles? And why is Jell-O the only palatable thing on my plate?

No one was happier than I to leave the hospital. The doctors, nurses and aides were cheerful and all, and I admire their dedication. But I know why a hospital is the kind of place people don't care to hang around. *(Oct. 1, 2000)*

IT'S ABOUT TIME THE GOVERNMENT TRIED TO TEST VARIETY OF DIETS

Finally.

The government has decided to take a look at a couple of the popular diets on the market to see if they work.

As one who has tried more diets than Bill Clinton has political lives, I can only say it's about time.

Those who know me know that I'm on a seemingly perpetual diet. I've always been on the heavy side. Some would suggest that I'm "big-boned," but I don't know that my bones are any bigger than anyone else's. It's what's around those bones that's my trouble.

My dieting goes back to my college days. My first diet — like some of those around these days — wasn't terribly healthy, as I recall. I drank lots of Tab — the bitter cola alternative offered by the Coke people in those days — and ate broiled fish. That was about it.

I lost lots of weight. But man does not live by Tab and fish alone, and within a year or two, I'd gained it all back.

About 10 years ago, the fad was liquid protein. That's the one that Oprah popularized by bringing a wagon of chicken fat on her program to show how much weight she'd lost by using the liquid protein diet.

The diet required you to drink several protein shakes a day and eat nothing. More than a diet, it was sort of a fast, with the shakes designed to make sure that you got proteins and vitamins.

Several of my larger journalistic colleagues went on that diet, with amazing results. Guys who had been quite large became small guys, almost overnight. That, I thought, was the diet for me.

So I got on the liquid protein diet and lost about 50 pounds within a couple of months.

Ultimately, though, I couldn't stay on that diet forever. When I'd go out to dinner with friends, they'd order meals, I'd order a glass of water to mix my protein shake. That got old fast. I'd ask my wife for a forkful of what she was having. One forkful led to a nibble, one nibble led to a taste, one taste led to a small plate. . . . Well, you can see where it went from there. I gained those 50 pounds back.

Perhaps the most successful diet that I ever went on wasn't a "diet" at all. Several years back I joined Weight Watchers. That organization tries to get you to change your lifestyle. I would go to meetings once a week, keep track of the calories that I ate each day, and pay close attention to my weight. I lost about 90 pounds with Weight Watchers.

But then, the excuses came. My life somehow got busier. I wasn't able to attend the sessions each week. I ended up eating out more often where I had less control of what I was eating. Then I had surgery. One thing led to another, and I started regaining weight.

I've managed to keep about 60 pounds off, but I'll be the first to say that I'd like to take off much more. It doesn't help me much that I like food, or that my favorites happen to be the foods that I should stay away from — things like pastries and baked goods, sweets, dairy products and the like. (I'm fascinated that Julia Child has lived to be 87 while cooking with all those creams and sauces over the years. Does she know something that doctors aren't telling the rest of us?)

The feds are going to study low-carbohydrate diets that are high in protein, and another that is ultra-low-fat and virtually vegetarian. I'll be eager to see the results.

I only wish they were also studying the pill that one company is touting these days that you're supposed to take before going to bed and then awaken the next day, miraculously thinner. I have doubts about that one — or any diet that claims that you can eat whatever you want as long as you take this, drink that or say a magic incantation before going to bed.

There probably is only one real answer to too much weight,

however: Eat less and exercise more.

Despite that, many will continue on the search for the ever-elusive "miracle diet," leading me to believe that P.T. Barnum's remarks about a sucker being born every minute were right on target. *(June 1, 2000)*

8-YEAR-OLD BOY AND HIS FAMILY CELEBRATE HIS SECOND CHANCE

Russell Witek is your average, curious, 8-year-old boy — and not incidentally a miracle of modern medicine.

Without a transplant using donated umbilical cord blood from the St. Louis Cord Blood Bank, Russell likely would not be with us today.

His story began four years ago, when Russell and his mother, Karen Witek, were attending a wedding rehearsal. Russell was to be the ring bearer the next day. At the rehearsal, Witek noticed her son coughing so much that he created a distraction.

The coughing persisted the next day and, even though the family was dressed for the wedding, Russell's father, Brian, thought it would be a good idea to see the doctor. A doctor looked at Russell, who was quite pale, suggested that he might be suffering from anemia or pneumonia and conducted some tests. The family then took Russell to the wedding, where he was very uncooperative. His mother had to bribe him with licorice to get him to walk down the aisle.

"He was really exhausted," Karen Witek said. "He did one dance on the dance floor, and he was wiped out."

The next day, the family — Brian, Karen and their older son, Garrett — took Russell back to the doctor to have blood drawn. Within hours, they learned that he was suffering from acute lymphoblastic leukemia, also known as ALL.

ALL is a rapidly progressing cancer of the blood that is

characterized by the overproduction of a form of white blood cell called a lymphoblast. The overproduction crowds the bone marrow, radically reducing the body's ability to form other normal and necessary blood cells.

The Witeks live in Geneva, Ill., about 40 miles west of Chicago. Russell was transferred to a hospital in Chicago, and the family made the trek.

Russell was in the hospital for four days and had a multitude of tests. He had a variety of spinal taps and marrow aspirations — a procedure where a needle is put into the pelvis and marrow is, in effect, plunged out — and was put on a 2 1/2-year course of chemotherapy. Thirty days after the leukemia was first diagnosed, it went into remission.

Russell continued with the chemotherapy, and his parents thought all was well. But when they took him to the doctor for his two-year checkup, they learned the worst — the leukemia had returned.

Doctors said that Russell would need a bone marrow transplant and that his chance for survival wasn't very good. Karen, Brian and Garrett all were typed, in hopes of being a match to give Russell the much-needed marrow. As it turned out, none of them matched.

Meanwhile, Russell had been placed on a national marrow donor registry, and the family soon learned that there were three bone marrow matches and one cord blood match. The cord blood match was from the St. Louis Cord Blood Bank at Cardinal Glennon Children's Hospital.

During pregnancy, the placenta and the blood within it serve as the lifeline of nourishment from the mother to the baby through the umbilical cord. Following the birth, the placenta, the cord and blood are usually discarded. But as a result of technology developed in the 1990s, doctors have learned that cord blood can serve as an alternative source of stem cells for stem transplantation and gene therapy. If parents are willing, delivering physicians collect the blood during the third stage of labor.

Umbilical cord blood is comparable to blood found in bone marrow. But unlike bone marrow blood, it can be frozen, stored and used later. Even better, it's often easier to match patients with umbilical cord blood than blood in bone marrow.

"You might explain it like a lottery," said Kathy Mueckl, nurse coordinator with the blood bank. "It's the difference between having to match six out of six numbers, and having to match only four out of six numbers. You get more winners when you only have to match four."

Though the use of some types of stem cells is in dispute these days, there's none when it comes to stem cells from cord blood. "We're approved by the pope, the president and everyone else," Mueckl said. "It's a way for a mother to give life twice."

The St. Louis Cord Blood Bank began collecting umbilical cord blood in 1996 and is now the second-largest program in the world.

The Witeks did their research on cord blood, and the more they learned, the more excited they were. "I kept saying, 'Wow! Cool!'" Karen Witek said.

The blood was shipped to Chicago, and in October 2000, Russell received a cord blood transplant at Children's Memorial Hospital there. He didn't bounce back immediately but gradually he returned to his normal self. "Now the biggest complaint he has is a flaky scalp," Witek said.

So thrilled is Witek that she has become practically an evangelist for cord blood transplants. "I approach virtual strangers and ask them to donate their cord blood," she said.

Earlier this month, Russell celebrated the second anniversary of his transplant. The family sang "Happy Transplant Anniversary to You," and he blew out candles.

The family continues to celebrate life.

= = = =

What you can give

* One person can save the lives of up to seven people by donating the following organs after death: heart, liver, lungs, kidneys, pancreas and small intestine.

* Living donors can provide blood, bone marrow, a kidney, a piece of the liver or a segment of a lung.

* One person can improve the lives of 40 to 50 people by donating after death skin, eyes, bone and soft tissue, heart valves, veins and arteries.

Source: Mid-America Transplant Services

= = = =

For information

Where to go for information about organ disease, transplants and donation.

* American Association of Kidney Patients, 1-800-749-2257, www.aakp.org

* American Association of Tissue Banks, 1-703-827-9582, www.aatb.org

* American Heart Association, St. Louis chapter, 314-367-3383, www.americanheart.org

* Children's Organ Transplant Association, 1-800-366-2682, www.cota.org

* American Liver Foundation, Missouri and Southern Illinois chapter, 314-352-7377 or 1-866-455-4837, www.liverfoundation.org

* The Living Bank, the nation's oldest and largest donor education group, 1-800-528-2971, www.livingbank.org

* National Marrow Donor Program, 1-800-627-7692, www.marrow.org

* Mid-America Transplant Services, the organization that distributes human organs and tissues in Missouri, Illinois and Arkansas, 314-991-1661, www.mts-stl.org

* National Minority Organ Tissue Transplant Education Program, 1-202-865-4888 or 1-800-393-2839, www.nationalmottep.org

* National Kidney Foundation of Eastern Missouri and Metro East, 314-961-2828 or 1-800-489-9585, www.nkfstl.com or www.kidney.org

* Eye Bank Association of America, 1-202-775-4999, www.restoresight.org

* The Coalition on Donation, an alliance of national transplant groups and local coalitions, 1-804-330-8620, www.shareyourlife.org

* National Transplant Assistance Fund, 1-800-642-8399, www.transplantfund.org

* St. Louis Cord Blood Bank, 1-314-268-2787

* Transplant Recipients International Organization Inc., 1-202-293-0980 or 1-800-874-6386, www.trioweb.org

* United Network for Organ Sharing, the organization that oversees the nation's organ allocation system. For transplant information, 1-888-894-6361; for a brochure on organ donation, 1-800-355-7427; www.unos.org *(Oct. 29, 2002)*

SUPPORT GROUP HELPS DAUGHTERS WHO'VE LOST THEIR MOTHERS

Katherine McGrory won't be celebrating Mother's Day today.

The 46-year-old executive from Des Peres was 9 when her mother died of cancer. Since that time, Mother's Day has always been painful for her.

"It's not like I hate the day or anything like that," said McGrory, who has no children. "I just try not to think about it. Mother's Day isn't the happiest day for me."

McGrory says she feels isolation and loneliness at times. She was her parents' only child, and although her father is alive, she often wishes she could speak with her mother and ask for advice once more.

But she also thinks her mother's death has made her stronger, more independent.

"My mom was gone," she said. "My father helped out, but I had to learn to do lots of things on my own."

McGrory's not alone. Many women whose mothers died when they were young feel a certain amount of loneliness. In a 1994 book, "Motherless Daughters: The Legacy of Loss," Hope Edelman discusses the unique problems of women who lose their mothers.

According to the book, common effects of early mother loss include feelings of loneliness, an overdeveloped sense of independence and self-reliance, and the belief that no one with a mother can understand what it means to have lost one.

As a result of the book, a nonprofit organization for women and girls has sprung up. It is called Motherless Daughters and is based in New York. The St. Louis chapter was scheduled to gather Saturday for a luncheon and remembrance program at the Salad Bowl restaurant in midtown.

Patricia Berne, the scheduled speaker, is a psychologist. She told me that the issue of women who lose their mothers is an important one.

"When women lose their mothers at an early age, at some point they are emotionally stuck at that point in time in which their mothers died," Berne said. "Many women often feel the need to go back and tell their mothers' story. Part of the reason for that is that when our mothers die, we lose the map for their life. We sometimes feel lost."

During holidays such as Mother's Day, some women may

feel inadequate, questioning whether they are good mothers.

"Sometimes, in the minds of these women, their mothers become larger than life, and they begin worrying whether they can live up to their mothers' expectations," Berne said. "Or, if they focus on their mothers in a negative sense, they have fears of becoming like their mothers."

Berne said women can deal with such issues by learning more about their mothers by talking with older relatives, friends and others who knew them.

"It's freeing to see your mother as a separate human being, with the same kinds of problems and insecurities we all have," she said.

Heather Caudill of St. Louis was 2 when her mother died.

"I guess I was too young to remember her, although sometimes I think I can," said Caudill, 27, a coordinator for the Alzheimer's Association.

Over the years, she's had difficulties because of her mother's death.

"When I was younger, it was very upsetting to have this feeling of difference," she said. "And now that I'm older, it's become worse. I've begun to realize how important mothers are in people's lives. I've begun missing things like shopping trips and other things that mothers and daughters do together, even dealing with the issues of mothers growing older."

Caudill says she's been greatly helped by getting involved with the Motherless Daughters group, which has support-group meetings every two weeks.

"It's really nice to know that you're not the only woman who feels this way," she said. "It's reaffirming to know that I'm not the only woman who occasionally fantasizes that her mother didn't actually die.

"I was having issues with losing my mother, and the Motherless Daughters group has been tremendously helpful in that."

The St. Louis chapter of Motherless Daughters can be reached by calling 862-6689. The national organization's Web site can be found at www.dfwnet.com/md. *(May 9, 1999)*

WITH TRIP, MAN, 72, SEEKS TO 'MOW DOWN' PROSTATE CANCER

Coast-to-Coast message.

Trevelyn Zander of Arnold has always been an adventurer.

Whether it's free-fall sky diving, rafting in Chile or walking across hot coals in Hawaii, Zander has always been willing.

Now he's embarking on what may be his biggest adventure yet: Today he begins a coast-to-coast trip — on a lawn tractor.

Zander, and his wife, Dorothy, want to call attention to prostate cancer and to raise money for cancer research.

Trevelyn, 72, was diagnosed with prostate cancer two years ago. He had his prostate removed and says he's feeling fine today.

"But I think a lot of people don't get the message about prostate cancer," he said. "I'm planning to take the message coast to coast."

The Zanders, along with their 95-pound malamute, Baby, will head out this morning. Trevelyn will drive the tractor. It will pull a small trailer with a sign that will read, "Help mow down prostate cancer with research and education."

Dorothy will follow, driving a Winnebago Grand Tour, for which the maker is providing fuel. Dorothy will keep an eye on Trevelyn. She would follow him, but at 7 mph, that's a bit slow for a Winnebago. So she'll let him drive ahead, start out later and check on him, and then move ahead, perhaps stopping for lunch or other diversions. "I plan to be no more than 20 miles away from him at all times," she said.

The Zanders know that they'd have troubles driving a lawn tractor on the interstate, so they plan to take back roads to reach their destinations. "We'll be passing through small towns, stopping and giving out literature," he said. "We'll talk to people, stay as long as makes sense, and then move on."

The first "major" destination will be Forest City, Iowa, a town of about 3,000 people that's approximately 500 miles from St. Louis. Winnebagos are made there, and the Zanders will be there at the time of the Winnebago Grand National Rally, an annual convention. "We thought that would be a good place to deliver the message," Trevelyn said.

From there, they will head west. "Pike's Peak or bust!" exclaims Trevelyn, who really plans to go there. Then Death Valley and on to the Pacific Ocean. The couple will then return to Arnold and then head east — to Washington and then New York. Trevelyn's hoping that someone who is sympathetic at the Empire State Building will let him take the lawn tractor to the top on a freight elevator.

The trip will cover a minimum of 3,500 miles, and the Zanders estimate that they'll be on the road for three months.

Although the Zanders are trying to raise money for prostate cancer research, they're accepting no money. Instead, they'll be handing out envelopes addressed to the Barnes-Jewish Hospital Foundation for Urology.

"We don't want to carry money around with us," Dorothy said. "We want to encourage people to donate to the foundation."

The Zanders are having fun with this, setting giving levels with some "rewards" for those who donate. Those who give $5,000 or more get to be "honorary tour directors" and are given the chance to accompany the Zanders — in their own cars. Those who give $500 will get a T-shirt saying "I know a guy who road a lawn tractor coast to coast," and a log of the trip that Dorothy is putting together.

While the Zanders are planning to have fun, they are serious about hoping to educate people about prostate cancer. "It's a very serious disease," said Trevelyn, whose brother also had it. "But it's something that men don't pay a lot of attention to. We're hoping that by doing this, something that's pretty different, we'll be able to draw attention to prostate cancer and encourage people to get tested and to get treatment."

Those who want to help the Zanders raise money for prostate cancer research can send checks to: Barnes-Jewish Hospital Foundation — Urology, 600 South Taylor Avenue, St. Louis, Mo. 63110-1035. The Zanders can be reached by e-mail at djzander@jcn1.com *(July 8, 1999)*

Part 5:

Our Life and Times

ON A TERRIBLE DAY, WE SHARE IN THE NATION'S DISBELIEF AND CONCERN

I was in my car Tuesday morning, on the way to a gas station, when I heard the news over the radio.

One minute, the radio host was talking about whether Michael Jordan would play basketball again; the next minute, he was reporting that a plane had crashed into one of the towers of the World Trade Center.

After I bought gas, the news broke that a second plane had crashed into the second tower of the building. Then, as if in a film with surprise twists and turns, the news flashes came, one after the other: A plane had crashed into the Pentagon; planes had been hijacked; one tower of the World Trade Center had collapsed, then the other.

What was happening? I wondered. I sat in disbelief, a sensation that I shared Tuesday with countless other St. Louisans.

* David Spiegel, a student at the University of Missouri at St. Louis, was among a clot of students crowded around a small, color television set up on the second floor of Lucas Hall.

"I can't believe it," Spiegel said. "This is incredible. I heard about it when I got to school. I never thought we'd see anything like this in our country. Is this going to mean World War III?"

* Chris Worle, a Web designer for Maring, Kanefield and Weissman, realized that something was wrong when he arrived for work in the Central West End about 8:45 a.m. "The Central West End is usually pretty busy at that time of morning, but there wasn't much action at all. There were a few cars. Everyone was huddled in coffee shops watching television, or talking on their cell phones."

Worle went to his computer but found that most of the news Web sites were busy. He looked at a television and saw pictures of the bombed towers. "It looked like something out of a 'Die Hard' movie," he said. "At first I was just shocked. Then I was sick to my stomach thinking about how many lives were lost. I'm still pretty shocked. It's pretty hard to go on with the day."

* In classroom after classroom, students worried what the day's events meant. At Parkway South High School, students were in a frenzy about rumors that a plane had crashed into a building in Pittsburgh. Several students had friends and relatives there.

They later learned that a plane had crashed about 80 miles southeast of Pittsburgh, but not in the city.

* Stephen Spencer heard the news while he was eating breakfast at Delmonico's, a restaurant on Delmar Boulevard near Euclid Avenue. "While it's an awful thing that happened, and I pray for all those people who died, all I could think of was how glad I am that I live in St. Louis," he said.

"I figure terrorists think about places like New York and Washington when they decide to attack. I suspect some of them don't even know St. Louis is here. And I'm glad of it."

* Gail Compton, a public information officer for the city, was getting dressed for work when she heard the news on the radio. "I went to the television and turned on the 'Today' show and was horrified at what I saw."

She called a friend to ask if she could believe what was happening. "While I was on the phone, I see this plane that looked like it was heading to the building, and then there was an explosion. Katie Couric said, 'Oh my God, I think that plane just hit the second tower.' It happened, right before my eyes."

Compton said she was glad to arrive at work. "This is the kind of thing where you want to share your feelings with other people," she said. "It was absolutely horrible, but I don't think the full impact of it hit me until a couple of hours later. I couldn't believe it."

* Mary Sanford had just dropped her daughter off at Gateway School when she happened to change channels on her radio to catch the news.

"I couldn't believe what I was hearing," she said. "It didn't seem real. I asked myself, 'Why? Why?'

"And then I did what I thought I should do — I prayed for all those who lost their lives. What a tragedy. What a tragedy."

Tragedies like this stay with us the rest of our lives. For one generation, that tragedy was Pearl Harbor. For another generation, it was the assassination of President John F. Kennedy. For this generation, Sept. 11, 2001, is a date that will live in infamy. *(Sept. 12, 2001)*

AFTER DAY OF HORROR, AMERICA BECOMES A DIFFERENT PLACE

Things have changed so much in the last seven days.

Before 7:48 a.m. last Tuesday, America was a different place. Our priorities, so important then, seem trivial today.

A week ago, Americans were still talking about Rep. Gary Condit and his involvement with missing intern Chandra Levy. Republicans were suggesting a cut in the capital gains tax, and Democrats were arguing that the tax cuts already enacted meant that the president would have to dip into Social Security funds.

Locally, St. Louisans were excited about Tiger Woods' arrival at Bellerive Country Club. Republicans were claiming irregularities in St. Louis County elections. City aldermen were squabbling over ward redistricting. Now, a week after terrorists hijacked four planes, targeted buildings in New York and Washington and killed thousands of innocent people, all of those issues that were so important last week seem much less important today.

Other news broke last week, but people barely noticed. Forest Park Forever and the St. Louis Parks Department said thanks but no thanks to a proposal to erect some gates and entrance markers to Forest Park.

Mayor Francis Slay announced he was talking with a Dallas-based developer Clear Channel Entertainment about renovating Kiel Opera House, which has been shuttered since 1991. Last week, this news merited only a few paragraphs in the newspaper.

We have vowed not to let the terrorists win, but in a way they are winning. As we are distracted from our routines, as we make air travel less convenient because of tightened security, as we talk of increasing governmental power to wiretap and monitor e-mail, we are giving up a bit of our freedom.

Gone also is the innocence of our children. What has happened is unnerving to many of them. Many parents and teachers have had to talk to their youngsters about terrorism and about wars.

All over St. Louis, children have been writing papers and poems about what has taken place. A friend shared this poem with me. It's by Adrienne Comage, 11, the daughter of Thomas and Michelle Comage, and a student at Our Lady of

Fatima School in Florissant.

This prayer is for those,
Who died without reason.
For those who went to work,
And never went home.
This is for the thousands of lives,
That were lost on that Day.
That terrible day that I will never forget ;
The Day that America was under attack.
This prayer is for the families,
Who lost the ones so dear,
The ones they loved
With all their hearts.
The ones who they will never see again.
This is for those,
Who suffered on that day.
The Day America was under attack.
This prayer is for those,
Who died helping others.
For those who dedicated their lives,
To helping those in need.
To the firemen and policemen,
Who tried so hard to save others,
And died,
On the Day America was under attack.
This prayer is for those,
Who did this deed.
What they did was wrong,
But they died, too.
They have families and friends,
Just as those who were innocent.
Even as the enemy here,

Their families are suffering in the same way.
This is for those who did that deed,
And put America under attack,
On that day.
We will come out of this. But we will be changed forever.
(Sept. 18, 2001)

DAUGHTERS CHERISH MEMORIES OF THEIR PARENTS' LOVE STORY

Henry Bennett didn't want to go to the party.

It had been set up by a friend of his, John Underwood. Bennett and Underwood had been childhood friends, growing up in the St. Louis area.

But Bennett never felt comfortable at parties. He didn't consider himself to be much of a social person, and he felt he always had to be "on" at such gatherings.

After considerable urging from Underwood, though, Bennett went to the party. That decision — in 1946 — was one he would never regret. At the party, Bennett's eyes were fixed on one woman. Dorothy Wilkerson was standing along a wall, tapping her foot to the music. Bennett, who had always been shy around women, summoned up the courage to walk over to Wilkerson and ask her to dance.

She accepted, and Bennett found this woman to be special. She liked to talk, she was attractive and she was funny. They danced to that song — and the next song, and the next.

Bennett was thrilled with this woman who smelled so nice. He invited her to a movie the next night, and she accepted. What had started out for Bennett as a reluctant appearance at a dance had turned into a courtship.

Within two years, Bennett and Wilkerson had decided to get married. But before that could happen, Bennett knew he had to win over Wilkerson's grandmother. Wilkerson's grandmother had raised her after her parents were killed in a car accident when she was 3.

Callie Blackman was strict. Whenever her granddaughter went out on a date, Blackman set a curfew, and waited up to make sure that Wilkerson got back on time. She grilled the young men who took her granddaughter out. She had decided that Bennett was "OK," but whether he was OK enough to marry her granddaughter was another story.

Bennett told her that he had a good job, working for the post office. He would take good care of Dorothy, he promised.

Blackman nodded approvingly, and the marriage took place.

As time went by, the Bennetts had three daughters. They doted on them, making sure the girls had everything they needed.

All the while, the love of Henry and Dorothy Bennett never faded. He nicknamed her "Baby Boo," and she called him "Shug," short for sugar. It wasn't uncommon for the girls to walk into a room and find their parents hugging or kissing. In a recent interview, daughter Katherine Bennett Brown said: "It made us feel good to know that they loved each other so much. I knew that if they loved each other so much, they loved us just as much."

The daughters all grew up, and Henry and Dorothy's love remained strong. They bought themselves a swing for their back porch, and they loved nothing better than sitting out there during the summer for hours at a time, talking about anything and everything.

As they grew older, Henry and Dorothy faced some illnesses. Both suffered from arthritis, and Dorothy had some heart problems. But they never let their ailments rule their lives. They coped with them the best they could, and they didn't complain to others when they didn't feel well. They may have confided in one another about how they were really feeling, but when someone else asked, they would always say that they were fine.

In 1998, their daughters held a 50th anniversary dinner to honor their parents, and I recently viewed a videotape of the event. When it came time for the couple to make remarks, Dorothy had tears in her eyes. "I love this man so much," she said. "He's always been the only one for me. Nobody else could ever take his place."

He said, "This is a wonderful woman, and I love her with all my heart." And then they hugged.

Their health continued to fail, and in October last year, Henry Bennett died. Three months later, Dorothy Bennett died.

"The doctors said she died of a heart attack," Katherine Bennett Brown said. But you'll never convince her of that.

"There's no question that my mother died of a broken heart." *(Feb. 21, 2002)*

HELPFUL MAN PROVIDES A SNAPSHOT OF HOW NICE PEOPLE CAN BE

Tiffany Wachter had only the best of intentions.

Wachter, of Des Peres, was the matron of honor at her sister's wedding recently, and offered to produce something special for the rehearsal dinner: a slide show of her sister and her fiance.

To put it together, Wachter went on a hunt-and-gather spree, searching for all sorts of photos of her sister and her sister's husband-to-be. "I got all kinds of pictures from his mom and from my mom and dad," Wachter said. "Pictures of him as a kid with Santa, his grade school pictures, all of her growing up pictures, including a picture with her sitting on the toilet wearing a sombrero — you know, all those embarrassing pictures that parents like to save forever."

Then from her sister she got all of the pictures of the couple taken since their first date. "I promised that I would take care of all these beloved pictures," Wachter said. "Needless to say, I was in possession of a whole lot of irreplaceable memories and quite worried at the prospect of leaving them to be made into slides."

But made into slides they were, and with no problems.

At the camera shop, Wachter picked up all 80 pictures and slides, and thanked the salesman. She walked to her car with her screaming 22-month-old son in one hand and her purse, his train, his toy bunny and the envelope of pictures in the other. She placed the envelope on her trunk, fastened her son into the car seat, handed him his bunny and reached down to pick up his train, which she had dropped. After giving him his train, she got into the car and drove away.

It wasn't until 15 minutes later, when she reached her mother's home, that she realized the pictures were not in the car with her.

"I have never been so hysterical in my entire life," she said. "I've been in car accidents, I've even had an entire electric traffic signal pole fall on my car when the truck turning next to me hooked the crossbar, but in each of those instances, a strange calm came over me. This time, though, it was sheer panic."

Wachter put her son back into the car and retraced her steps, shaking all the way, praying that she would somehow find the pictures. With the help of some friendly salespeople, she scoured the parking lot, but there was nothing.

She returned to her mother's home and suddenly got a glimmer of hope. Her name and phone number had been on the envelope. Could someone have called her?

She checked her messages at home and, sure enough, a man named Don "Russ" Russell had left a message. He said that he had been across the street from the camera store and saw her drive away. Two or three cars had driven over the envelope, and he had walked over to see what was in it. When he saw that they were old photos, he told her, he figured they were pretty important and she would want them back.

"I went home right away," Wachter said. "When I got there, the phone was ringing and it was him. He said he thought he had them all and told me how to get them back."

Wachter was thrilled. She thanked Russell profusely and gave him $100. "At that point, I would have given him my car if I'd had a way home," she said. "I was that happy."

Later, at dinnertime, Wachter's doorbell rang. To her surprise, it was Russell. He told her that he couldn't take the $100, and handed it back to her in an envelope.

In the envelope was a note that read, simply: "I appreciate your generosity, but cannot accept the money. I do things like this in hopes that someday when I need help, someone will be there. If you feel so compelled, donate this money to a worthy charity. Thank you, Russ."

Wachter says Russell has given her faith in mankind.

Wachter's not sure if Russell is an angel. "But," she says, "he's certainly earned points in heaven as far as I'm concerned."
(Oct. 9, 2001)

HIPPIES AND HIP CHECKS: A RESTAURANT AND AN OLD RINK SLIDE INTO RETIREMENT

My son and I visited a soon-to-be-defunct institution last week to reminisce about a soon-to-be-defunct institution.

Will and I ate dinner at Sunshine Inn. For those of you who somehow never heard of it, Sunshine Inn was perhaps the best bastion of vegetarian food in the region.

Well, it started out as a vegetarian restaurant. Later it added fish and chicken. Most of the food on the menu, however, continued to be vegetarian.

Ken Cooper, a fellow Washington University student, took me there for the first time in the 1970s. He was on a vegetarian kick at the time and insisted that I go with him to the restaurant. A fellow student, Rudy Nickens, was an owner of the place, and Ken had learned about it through him.

Being a dyed-in-the-wool meat eater, I was somewhat reluctant. But Ken insisted, and I went. The food was great. The atmosphere was greater. It had sort of a peace-and-love atmosphere about it. This was the '70s, mind you, and the clientele here was an interesting, eclectic group that ranged from writers to hippies. Some were both.

I remember I ordered vegetarian fried rice and fell in love with the place. In those days, the restaurant had no sugar, just honey, and I remember being disappointed when I tried to mix honey into my iced tea. But everything else was good. I was hooked.

Over the years, my wife and I ate there often. When Will was born, we brought him with us, too. We liked going there for brunch, to enjoy their turkey sausage and the fresh, hot rolls they served.

As we sat there last week, Will munching on his chicken tenders and me downing a cup of vegetarian chili, it was as if we were visiting an old friend for the last time. The restaurant is closing Sunday, and we're going to miss it.

The building was bought by developer Pete Rothschild, who wants higher rent for the place. Sunshine Inn will be no more, to be replaced by a Latin-themed restaurant called Babaloo's. Nickens and co-owner Martha McBroom have no plans to open another restaurant elsewhere.

So as we sat there eating our last supper, we thought about

another friend that was soon to be no more.

Mayor Clarence Harmon last week announced plans to tear down The Arena, after trying to find a redeveloper for it. A couple of competing aquarium ideas had been floated, but they sank when the proposed developers were unable to get financing. The mayor has a company on the hook that will build offices there and provide 500 jobs.

It's too bad that The Arena has to go, but it's costing the city $50,000 a month just to keep it standing. It makes sense, sadly, to tear it down.

Will took a bite of his Caesar salad, and I wolfed down my tofu fried rice, as we thought about the times we'd visited The Arena.

I vividly remembered my first visit to the big barn on Oakland Avenue. It was the early 1960s, and my dad took me to see the Three Stooges at the Police Circus. I was thrilled to see Larry, Moe and Curly Joe, who by then were up in age, along with Captain Eleven, a children's television character who had hosted a daily barrage of Three Stooges clips on Channel 11.

Will remembered his first visit there, too. It was when he was about 4, and Elizabeth and I had taken him there to see "Sesame Street Live." He recalled that he'd also seen "Disney on Ice" there.

We also remembered that I had taken him there to see his first and only Blues hockey game. Longtime readers may recall a column I wrote about that once. I knew absolutely nothing about hockey, and it was the first time I'd ever even tried to watch a full game. The Blues won that night, with a score of what I had thought was 35-30. We found out later that the score had been 3-2. I had been following the scoreboard for shots on goal.

By now, Will was finishing his apple pie, and I was polishing off what was to be my last purple cow, a drink made up of frozen yogurt and grape juice.

We made our peace with our dying friends, Sunshine Inn and The Arena. We understand why both have to go, but it makes us no happier.

It's hard to say goodbye to an old friend. *(April 26, 1998)*

DARING TO MESS WITH SUPERMAN

What's the super deal?

First, DC Comics announces its plan to kill off Superman, causing serious consternation at my home.

Not only is my son the world's biggest Superman fan, with comic books, games and figures galore, but his old man is no slouch either.

When I was a kid, you'd find me around the television set every afternoon at 5 p.m., waiting for my favorite hero to come on.

Faster than a speeding bullet! More powerful than a locomotive! Able to leap tall buildings at a single bound! "Look! Up in the sky! It's a bird! It's a plane! It's Superman!"

Yes, Superman! Amazing being from another planet who can change the course of mighty rivers! Bend steel in his bare hands! And who, disguised as Clark Kent, mild-mannered reporter for a great metropolitan newspaper, fights a never-ending battle for truth, justice and the American way!

How great it would be to be invincible and have such powers that no one can ever hurt you, I thought. Not to mention being able to fly anywhere you want to go at any time.

Being able to go wherever you want — whether you fly or not — is a big deal when you're 9 years old and generally restricted to your own back yard. Maybe that had something to do with my admiration of the man from Krypton.

My 12-year-old son, Will, and I have done such things as

traveled to Metropolis, Ill., to see the famous Superman statue there and visited comic book conventions in search of classic Superman books.

So you can imagine how disturbed we were when DC decided to kill Superman.

Surely they'll bring him back, we thought.

No, no, they insisted. He's dead for good.

Well, that was it. Our hero was going to be killed. The least we could do was to buy the comic book in which he was to die.

Apparently, millions of other Americans felt the same way we did, and that book was hard to find. Finally, a newspaper colleague who is also a Superman fan found a copy of the book (in which Superman is killed off by a character named Doomsday) and got one for Will. He's preserved it, putting it in a special plastic bag.

So now we've got a super beef.

DC has turned around and has decided to bring Superman back from the dead in "Adventures of Superman," No. 500. Everyone was fooled. We bought every collector's item imaginable and the Man of Steel is still around.

And, if that wasn't enough, we're now learning that he's not coming back as Clark Kent, "mild-mannered reporter for a great metropolitan newspaper."

Oh, nooooo.

This time, he's returning variously as a cyborg (half-man, half-machine), a steel-worker, a teen-ager and a cold-blooded super-being. Readers won't know which one is the real Superman until an issue that will be printed in August.

Give us a break!

I guess it's fine to kill Superman off occasionally. Since he was created in 1938 by Joe Shuster and Jerry Siegel, a couple of youngsters in Cleveland, Superman has probably been killed and brought back to life more times than Ross Perot has been on television. But he's almost always been killed and brought back in the same issue, bringing a sigh of relief to his fans who worried that the man "who came to Earth with powers and abilities far beyond those of mortal men" would be lost to us forever. To kill him off, leave him dead for months and then bring him back in some form other than his natural self seems, well, unseemly.

I suppose I should be glad. Superman's somehow risen from the grave, here on Earth to fight crime once more. But it would be a whole lot easier if he just came back as Clark Kent. The writers of Superman could have taken a cue from the writers of the old "Dallas" program: We could have learned that Superman's death was just a dream.

Oh, well. That obviously won't happen. So, we continue along, wondering what will happen.

For magazine executives who want to drum up circulation, this whole thing has been a great idea. It's a return to the concept of the old movie serials of the 1930s and 1940s, which kept people returning to movie theaters week after week to find out what would happen to their favorite hero. It's turned DC Comics around. Before Superman's death the company was slipping badly. Since that time, however, it's become the top comics publishing company in the country.

But for readers like me, it's been something akin to water torture.

Maybe I ought to get a more relaxing hobby. *(April 30, 1993)*

TIME TAKES ITS TOLL ON HOWARD JOHNSON'S, BUT NOT ON MEMORIES

Been to a Howard Johnson's restaurant lately? Better hurry. They're going the way of the drive-in theater.

Howard Johnson's restaurants used to dot America's landscape, like A&P grocery stores. They were in cities and along America's highways. Now they're slowly fading away.

When I was a kid, my dad rarely took us out to dinner, but when he did, the family would pack into his old Chrysler and go to Howard Johnson's on North Kingshighway, near Natural Bridge Avenue. I'd notice the familiar orange roofs, the signs that featured "Simple Simon" and the "pieman," the thick white coffee cups, the 28 flavors of ice cream. I'd always order my favorite, the "tendersweet clams," and my little sister would order the fried shrimp. And there was always hot apple crisp topped with ice cream for dessert.

When I was in college, friends and I would sometimes head to the Howard Johnson's on Clayton Road for its all-you-can-eat specials. Several times we tried to eat enough to close the place down.

But fewer people are able to enjoy those experiences these days. The Howard Johnson's on Kingshighway closed years ago, first becoming a paint store, then a Kentucky Fried Chicken restaurant, before being boarded up and abandoned.

The HoJo's on Clayton Road is now a Layton's restaurant.

In fact, the only Howard Johnson's restaurant left in the entire state of Missouri — indeed, the only one west of the Mississippi — is in Kirkwood, at 1130 South Kirkwood Road.

The first restaurant was opened in Massachusetts in 1925 by 27-year-old Howard Deering Johnson as a small patent medicine store with a soda fountain. Johnson developed a variety of ice cream flavors, doubling the amount of butterfat traditionally used in ice cream in those days. The place became a hit.

By 1965, Howard Johnson's was the nation's largest restaurant chain. Kentucky Fried Chicken, Burger King, even McDonald's, were all small potatoes compared to Howard

Johnson's. By the late '70s, Howard Johnson's had more than 1,000 restaurants and 500 motels.

But the times were changing. Fast-food franchises were taking over. Instead of going to restaurants for leisurely breakfasts, lunches and dinners, Americans were becoming more accustomed to eating on the run. Today, only 15 Howard Johnson's restaurants remain in the nation.

The chain sit-down restaurants like Applebee's, Chili's and Outback have found a niche by appealing to a younger crowd than HoJo's.

Despite the trend, managers at the Kirkwood Howard Johnson's see a future for themselves. General manager Buddy Fresta told me that the restaurant was working on a concept to keep many of the old favorites, like the clams, hot dogs and shakes, and combine them with more contemporary cuisine. "Our goal is to be around for a long time," Fresta said. "We want to bring the restaurant into the 2000s. We hope to keep our older clientele while bringing in younger people."

Right now, the restaurant does a great breakfast business, Fresta said. "But the dinner crowd is where we hurt. The older clientele doesn't like to go out much at night. That's why we're going to be trying to attract younger diners as well."

Still, there's something special about the old-fashioned places. They don't resort to waiters and waitresses in funny hats and outfits. They're not trying to be hip with catchy songs and trendy food. When you go to a Howard Johnson's, you know what you're going to get. There's something comforting about that.

"I used to love them as a kid growing up," said Barrett Williams, who dined at the Kirkwood restaurant with his mother on Friday. "They were always good places. They've always been quintessential American dining."

Here's hoping Buddy Fresta's successful in keeping St.

Louis' only Howard Johnson's going. I'd hate to see an American tradition disappear. *(April 23, 2002)*

THERE'S NOTHING FOR MISSOURIANS TO FEAR WHEN THEY CROSS THE RIVER

Some Missourians have never been there in their lives. Others caution their friends to beware if they go. Still others give it names like "over there." Beware, Missourians warn one another.

This scary place, this frightening destination, is Illinois. No, we don't mean Chicago. True, it's in Illinois, but to us Missourians, that's "different."

No, we're talking about the Metro East area, across the Mississippi River.

For whatever reason, many Missourians are frightened to death of it.

Some St. Louisans absolutely refuse to cross the river, as if the Poplar Street Bridge is somehow the entrance to hell.

Most recently, the Metro East area became a topic of discussion when the Cardinals were trying to get the Missouri Legislature to support a new downtown stadium. In the debate, some mentioned the possibility that the Cardinals might consider moving to Illinois.

Impossible, lots of St. Louisans said. Why would the Cardinals move to Illinois? It's too dangerous. No one from Missouri would go there to watch the games.

That must have come as quite a surprise for Metro East folks, who live, work and play there all the time.

We Missourians tend to forget that Illinoisans cross the bridge all the time to come to St. Louis. And not just for ballgames. Folks in the Metro East area seem to be more willing to visit St. Louis than vice versa for all sorts of events.

Part of the fear of Illinois, I'm sure, is that St. Louisans sometimes have a myopic view of the Metro East area. When we think Illinois, we think of East St. Louis, a place that seems to be a favorite spot for people who dump bodies.

What we often forget, however, is that quite often, murders are committed in Missouri and taken across the river for dumping. That being the case, you could argue that Illinoisans have more reason to be frightened of coming to Missouri — where the crimes are taking place. And East St. Louis has much less crime than some people believe.

Besides, what we often forget, is that the Metro East is a vast area. It's not even all in one county. St. Clair and Madison counties about evenly divide up the people, with some spillover to Monroe, Clinton, Jersey and others. The area is home to more than 600,000 people.

I had the opportunity to learn about the Metro East early in my journalism career. In the late '70s, I was a reporter for the Belleville News-Democrat. My first assignment was to cover the towns of Troy, Glen Carbon and St. Jacob. Not exactly scary places.

Missourians who refuse to cross the river don't know what they're missing. It's a beautiful part of the country. The northern part of the area features breathtaking river bluffs. The magnificence of the Clark Bridge is truly a sight to see. The country roads throughout the area give you a real view of what makes up the Metro East.

But even the scenery isn't enough to lure some Missourians. Joan, a friend of mine, refuses to go.

"You couldn't pay me enough money to go over there," she said. "I just don't feel safe. Maybe it's silly of me, but I'm not interested in going over there."

Jim Pennekamp chuckled when asked about the fear some Missourians have of the Metro East area. "But it doesn't really surprise me," said Pennekamp, executive director of the Leadership Council of Southwestern Illinois.

Pennekamp said that some 70,000 folks from Illinois cross the river to work each day. Some 30 percent to 40 percent of those working downtown are Illinoisans, he said.

There are lots of old perceptions by Missourians of what's across the river. "But I think the dynamic is changing. Developments like MetroLink and the Casino Queen are starting to bring people over who have never been here before," he said. "And I think those who have developed the courage to actually cross the river have found their experiences to be most enjoyable."

Still, Pennekamp acknowledges that the Metro East may as well be a foreign land to some Missourians, who somehow think that it's far, far away.

"A joke over here, when we invite our Missouri friends over for dinner, is to start dinner 45 minutes early," he said. "Inevitably, Missourians get here and look at their watches, wondering how they got here so quickly." *(June 16, 2002)*

LEADERSHIP PROGRAM GETS CUT BECAUSE IT WON'T AID TEST SCORES

With the end of school desegregation comes the apparent passing of a program that has helped bring hundreds if not thousands of students together while training them in leadership and team building.

The Metropolitan Student Leadership Program is being axed by the St. Louis School Board. The program was funded with school desegregation money. With desegregation going by the wayside, the program is getting the heave-ho.

In a way, you can't blame the St. Louis School Board. They're under intense pressure to achieve, and achievement for most people means rising scores. With deseg money drying up, the school district's got to make some decisions.

It's too bad, though. The program was a good one. It brought kids of different races together and taught them important lessons like teamwork. It brought together students from 21 schools from the city and St. Louis County through projects like wilderness weekends, community service, living history projects, orienteering and urban exploration projects. It was the kind of program that private schools offer all the time.

Teachers in the program enhanced the curriculum, making it come alive.

For instance, one assignment required students to take MetroLink to Union Station. While there, students had different assignments that they had to accomplish while staying on schedule. One student wore a bandanna over his eyes and reported back to his group what it was like to be a person with a disability. Another was given one dollar for lunch in a lesson on how to budget.

Each assignment taught a lesson, and was fun for the students at the same time.

To no one's surprise, the students loved the program. In a booklet put together by students of the program a couple of years ago, students all but gushed about it.

Wrote one: "MSLP has taught me to set realistic goals. By 'realistic,' I don't mean setting simple goals just because they are easily attained. For me, setting realistic goals means setting goals for myself that may seem rather difficult to obtain, but are a physical and mental possibility. The program has helped me to realize that I can do so much more than I ever thought I could do. It has helped me to build confidence in my ability to get things accomplished."

And, in an unusual move, several teachers involved in the program made an unsuccessful but impassioned last-ditch plea before the School Board to save the program.

A program this good surely deserves funding. But the school system makes a point as well.

"We had to make some hard decisions," said Charles Brown, an associate superintendent. "We're getting down to the bare necessities. We've had to ask ourselves to what degree will programs we keep improve test scores. Based on criteria that we set after consulting with teachers, students and parents, the program didn't score high on the list of priorities. The most important issue was whether it would affect students' scores."

Brown was quick to add that the decision was no reflection on the program's quality or whether it was a popular one. "I used to be director of the program, and I know it was important and helped kids. But it wasn't a priority."

Brown added, however, that Superintendent Cleveland Hammonds has promised to try to keep a component of the program in the summer school curriculum.

The money is tight, and St. Louisans are screaming for better test scores. Brown makes a good point in defending the position to shut down the program.

Still, it would be nice if some company or foundation came along with the money to save it.

The program's work isn't the sort that shows up in test scores. But it often materializes in other ways, by producing better citizens. And that's something our community should be willing to invest in. *(July 29, 1999)*

'ROCK' CHOIR IS READY TO ROLL IN PERFORMANCE FOR POPE

Keeping the faith.

Malcolm Speed was almost disbelieving when he got the news back in September.

Speed, a minister of music at St. Alphonsus "Rock" Catholic Church who directs the church's Voices of Praise choir, was told by the Rev. Maurice Nutt that the group had been asked to perform as part of this week's papal festivities.

"Everyone in the choir was excited," he said. "But we didn't want to get too excited, just in case they changed their mind about us being there."

But no one changed their minds, and Monday night, the Voices of Praise held their final rehearsal at the church at 1118 North Grand Boulevard before a scheduled performance Wednesday morning. Also performing will be the Voices of St. Alphonsus, the church's larger and better-known choir.

"I never ever dreamed that I would perform for the pope," said Speed, 48. "I've never performed before anyone like that. No one even close. I think the biggest person I've ever performed for was during a convention where Dr. Thomas Dorsey was present." The late Dorsey was known as the dean of gospel music.

The enthusiasm among choir members has been growing steadily, even though the choir has tried to keep its excitement in check. A visit to the church by CBS television on Sunday only increased the excitement.

Speed is especially excited because the choir will sing a song that it performed on a CD it released last year. The song, "What Worship Is," was written by Kyle Kelley, and it will be sung right after an early-morning call for worship.

The choir held its only rehearsal at the Trans World Dome last week. "That kind of added to the excitement," Speed said. "That place is huge.

"I've been playing for St. Alphonsus for almost eight years. I know there was a time in the past when the choir had gone to Rome, but I never, ever expected anything like this. Just the fact that we're going to perform for 100,000-plus people is amazing. And to be featured at something like this — well, it's something beyond your wildest dreams."

I had a chance to hear Speed and the Voices of Praise perform last week during a special program at St. Charles Borromeo Catholic Church. The choir's enthusiasm was infectious. As Speed put his all into the direction, the choir's voices filled the church, causing even the most staid members of the church to clap their hands to the music. I'll be surprised if the same doesn't happen Wednesday.

Speed said he was awed by the security involved in the pope's visit. The Secret Service is working on the security detail to ensure the Holy Father's safety. "We all had to submit our Social Security numbers, I guess to make sure that we weren't the kind of people who would threaten a pope," Speed said. "We're clear."

To get to Wednesday's performance, the choir will have to leave the parish at 1:30 a.m. to board buses. Choir members won't leave the Dome before noon on Wednesday.

To help the choir and make sure that no one misses the bus, the church has invited choir members to sleep there tonight. Videos and food will be provided, along with a place for members to curl up for a few hours of sleep.

But Speed, a self-described night person, doesn't plan to do any sleeping. "I'm just going to stay up all night and fool my body into thinking it's still Tuesday night," he said.

When the choir is finally allowed to leave the Dome, Speed knows exactly what he's going to do: "I'm going to go home and go to bed," he said.

While the rest will be much deserved, it won't be for long. During the first week in February, the choir will be headed to Huntsville, Ala., to perform there.

"We're a busy choir, and we'll be busy during the pope's visit, but thank God for it," he said. "We could be sitting at church doing nothing. It's a real honor to be able to perform.

And to be able to perform at something like this, well, it's a true blessing.

"For me, it's a sign that faithfulness does pay off. I just hope St. Louisans will keep us in their prayers." *(Jan. 26, 1999)*

ON THIS 4TH OF JULY, CELEBRATE, PROTECT OUR NATION'S FREEDOMS

Independence Day 2002.

While we barbecue today, enjoy fireworks, or spend time with friends and loved ones, it's probably also a good time to think about what we've got.

We live in a nation that offers us freedoms that we would not have if we lived most anywhere else. And though those freedoms have been harder to come by for some than for others, they are an ideal for which we collectively strive.

We argue forcefully in this country. We protest. We carry signs and debate with one another until we're exhausted.

But we have the right to speak out, and no one is going to arrest us for it. We know that unless we're violent, we can protest.

All of those rights weren't always guaranteed to all Americans — women and blacks, for instance. But those rights are promised to everyone these days.

It's important to realize, however, that not long ago our government — which was sworn to uphold the laws, including the Constitution and the Bill of Rights — trampled on those documents instead.

We shouldn't forget, for instance, that J. Edgar Hoover abused his power as the head of the FBI for years, choosing to use the office to intimidate the powerful and average citizens alike.

From 1956 to 1971, Hoover operated Cointelpro, a counterintelligence program that was shut down because of significant abuses of the First and Fourth amendments. Hoover's FBI infiltrated, monitored and targeted lawful organizations and their members. Hoover conducted secret wars against those citizens he considered threats, or whom he wanted to intimidate. Individuals whom most Americans consider heroes today — the Rev. Dr. Martin Luther King Jr., for instance — were targets of Hoover's intimidation efforts.

Today, because of potential terrorist attacks, some Americans are willing to forgo the freedoms that our founding fathers established for us.

If U.S. Attorney General John Ashcroft gets his way, you no longer will have to break the law to warrant an investigation by the feds. Ashcroft has released new surveillance guidelines that remove the protections against excesses by the FBI that were put in place years ago. The new guidelines make it easier for the FBI to snoop on people in churches, mosques, libraries, political groups, or Internet chat rooms, without even a hint of criminal or terrorist activity.

Ashcroft is telling Americans, in so many words: We're from the government. Trust us.

This shouldn't be a partisan issue. The protections against FBI intrusions were written under President Gerald Ford, a Republican.

As some seek to reign in our freedoms, it's important for us to realize that some of these changes could have a significant impact on our free exercise of religion and freedom of assembly, along with our right to express our political beliefs.

And though some Americans may consider such encroachments OK under the current administration and circumstances, it's important to remember that they could continue for generations. We should be able to have security without throwing away the Bill of Rights.

So as we're basting that first rib today, having good times with friends and relatives, or enjoying the fireworks display at the riverfront, let's take just a moment to remember what this holiday is about: a celebration of our freedoms and our independence. It's what makes the United States special. It's why very few of us would actually renounce our citizenship and live elsewhere. It's why so many long to immigrate here, and why many consider this to be the greatest nation in the world.

We're far from perfect. But there is much that is good about our country. Keeping that in mind, we should always resolve to maintain our liberties, and do what we can to prevent others from taking them from us, no matter what reason.

The Founding Fathers would have expected nothing less. *(July 4, 2002)*

Part 6:

Wit and and Wisdom

ANOTHER SHOCK CHALLENGES MY BOYISH SELF-IMAGE

I rarely watch myself on television.

I host a program on Channel 9 — "Mosaic" — but the show is taped in advance. Since I already know what everyone is going to say, I usually don't watch the show again when it's aired.

But a couple of weeks ago, my wife was watching the show, and I joined her. When the camera angle turned a certain way, I realized something: I'm balding at the crown of my head.

It's not something that I can see in the mirror each morning. But there it was — my scalp peeking through my hair in the back.

My first thought was that there was something wrong with the camera. Maybe the light in the studio was shining from an odd angle. Some flaw in the equipment.

I turned to my wife. "Am I balding in the back?"

"Sure you are," she said.

I was in shock. How could this be? I've never been the world's most handsome guy, but I always knew that I could count on my hair.

Since my freshman year in high school, when I begged and pleaded with my parents to let me grow an Afro (after a year of urging, they finally let me grow my hair a half inch), I've been concerned about my hair.

By my senior year in college, perhaps in a move of independence, I grew my hair about four inches long and let my beard grow to the point that I looked like I should be on the street with a sign that said "Will work for food."

Over the years, I cut my hair shorter and shorter. All was well until the end of the 1980s. I hadn't hit my mid-30s yet, and my hair was starting to gray. Insisting to myself that I was prematurely gray, I tried a few of the hair coloring products for men. The first one I tried made my head burn. That wouldn't do, so I tried a different one. This one worked, and for about two years I had black hair.

After a while, though, I came to realize that a little gray in my hair wasn't that bad. In fact, I thought, it gave me a mature appearance, something that I thought made me look as if I had more experience than my 35 years.

With the exception of growing a beard a few years later, I've virtually remained unchanged hairwise for the past 10 years.

But now this. Losing my hair. Not one of my friends bothered to tell me. No one sent me "hey baldy" letters. No jokes. Nothing. Just a surprise when I sat down to watch TV one day.

I used to bug my 20-year-old son about cutting his hair. He wears dreadlocks that are longer each time I see him. But no more. What I wouldn't give to have some of that hair on the back of my head.

I mentioned my new crisis to a friend of mine, who suggested that I cut all my hair off. That way, he reasoned, not only would people not know that I have gray hair, they'll also think that I'm being fashionable. Bald heads are the in thing now, he said.

That might be a good idea for someone else, but not for me. I have a funny shaped head. When I was a kid and wore my hair short, the other kids would tease me because of a valley in the middle of my head. That wasn't a lot of fun, and I don't think I want to go through it again (although it would be difficult for me to imagine adults yelling, "Here comes the big valley" as I walked by).

On top of that, I've never really understood the care and feeding of the bald dome. Yes, some people come by them naturally, but for those who shave their heads, how does that work? Do they shave their heads every day? How do you avoid missing spots in the back? Do you get a 5 o'clock shadow, and how do you handle that? Do you shine your head after you shave it?

Too many questions for me to consider.

I guess I'll just have to live with my balding head and gray hair.

I still think they're premature. *(Oct. 2, 2001)*

IT WAS SO HOT HERE THAT WE MAY AS WELL JOKE ABOUT IT

St. Louis is not the place to be at this time of year.

Hades would be a comforting relief.

Don't get me wrong. I love this place. In many ways, St. Louis for me is the perfect place to live.

Except in summer.

This is one hot place. St. Louis summers can be unbearable without air conditioning.

Our parents never worried about air conditioning. When I was growing up, my folks never complained about the heat. They'd get out an old, heavy, black electric fan and enjoy the hot breeze blowing around.

But today, many of us are wimps. We'll do whatever we

can to be where there's air conditioning.

Can you blame us? We don't even have the excuse Arizona has. You know, "It's hot, but it's a dry heat."

There's nothing dry about St. Louis heat. It's head-mopping, sweat-dripping, handkerchief-squeezing hot here.

Even the weathercasters aren't helping. I live in the city, and lately they've been saying that heat warnings are being issued for the city but not elsewhere. How's that? Does the heat know when it's hit the city limit?

I called KMOV-TV's chief meteorologist, Kent Ehrhardt. I figured I could count on Kent for an explanation.

He told me that a heat warning is issued when you have at least three days where the heat index is 105 degrees or more, or a single day when it reaches 115 degrees.

"Because the city has all this concrete, in addition to heat being generated by lots of buildings, the city sometimes has higher temperatures," he said. "And some of the city's brick buildings become ovens."

How hot is it in St. Louis?

It's so hot in St. Louis, the birds are using potholders to pull worms out of the ground.

It's so hot in St. Louis, a man walked by saying, "I wish we'd have a cooling-down rainstorm. ... It's not for me, you know; I've seen one. But for my 8-year old."

It's so hot in St. Louis, two trees were seen chasing a dog.

It's so hot in St. Louis, drivers are deciding that the best parking spot isn't necessarily the one in front of a building but the one with the most shade.

It's so hot in St. Louis that carrots are cooking underground, and all you have to do is pull them up and add salt and pepper.

It's so hot in St. Louis, you can burn an egg on the sidewalk.

It's so hot in St. Louis, we've stopped associating the Poplar Street Bridge with water.

It's so hot in St. Louis, the biggest fear of bicyclists is, "What if I get knocked out and end up on the pavement and burn to death?"

It's so hot in St. Louis, the best way to find it on a newspaper weather map is to look for that burnt orange section in the middle.

It's so hot in St. Louis, Zoo officials are feeding the birds crushed ice to keep them from laying hard-boiled eggs.

It's so hot in St. Louis, a police officer was chasing a street robber — and they were both walking.

It's so hot in St. Louis, car dealers are talking about their "not-so-hot" deals.

It's so hot in St. Louis, people sunbathing in Forest Park aren't bringing their sunscreen, they're bringing their dental records.

It's so hot in St. Louis, scientists recently detected beads of sweat on the statue of King Louis IX.

It's so hot in St. Louis, people are mopping up their patio furniture.

It's so hot in St. Louis, firefighters are opening the hydrants to take showers.

It's so hot in St. Louis, service station stops are measured by bottles of water rather than the need for gas.

It's so hot in St. Louis that I may punch the next person who says, "Hot enough for you?" *(July 23, 2002)*

RINGING IN THE NEW : CARS DON'T FLY YET, BUT WE'RE MUCH BETTER OFF

What a difference 100 years makes; 876,600 little hours...
A century.
Wow.

Here we are, in the 21st century.

It's not at all how I had imagined it.

When I was in the eighth grade, a teacher gave us an assignment to write about life in the year 2000. This was 1970, and the idea of life in the 21st century seemed so far off, so futuristic.

But I let my imagination go. Like many baby boomers, I'd been weaned on "The Jetsons," so flying cars were a natural. Cars would fly to their destinations. Even better, people would no longer drive them. They would just tell the car where they wanted to go, sit back and be delivered to their destinations as they read the paper or drank a cup of coffee.

People would no longer be overweight, either, because we wouldn't eat food. Instead, we'd take pills alone for our nutrition.

The world would finally have learned to live in peace and harmony, I wrote, and wars would be a thing of the past, found only in history books. The same would be the case for racial strife. Everyone would have equal rights, and blacks and whites would live together, with differences in skin color being no more important than differences in hair color or eye color.

I had other ideas as well, like buildings that would hover instead of being attached to the ground, although I can't recall now what the advantage of that was supposed to be.

Now here we are, on the first day of the first year of the new millennium. My car doesn't fly. My house doesn't hover. I'm not taking pills instead of eating food, although a look at my girth might make you think that wouldn't be a bad idea. We've still got wars. And we've still got racial tension.

But while the year 2000 hasn't lived up to my childhood expectations, there's no question that the world has changed drastically since 1900, the last time our year ended with two zeros.

Someone materializing here from 100 years ago would be amazed at all of the changes. Aside from the most obvious — automobiles have changed trips that once took hours to mere minutes, computers have given us access to information all over the world — lots of other changes have taken place.

Ours is a much more sanitary place than ever before. Indoor plumbing was a novelty in 1900. Daily bathing wasn't common. Deodorant? Fuhgedaboutit. Cleanliness in food preparation wasn't common. And antibiotics hadn't been developed yet. Ours was a pretty dirty and smelly place.

While some think that race relations today are worse than ever, few can recall firsthand how bad they were at the turn of the 20th century. Society in general opposed the idea of equal rights for blacks, and that opposition was backed up by laws that granted African-Americans second-class status. Interracial marriage was not only an affront to decency in those days, but in most states was a punishable offense. Lynching was an all-too-common occurrence.

The idea of equal rights for women was equally frowned upon in 1900. The idea that women could ever lead major corporations or play significant roles in business was an alien concept.

We've come a long way since 1900.

Chances are, we'll come even further — and faster — in the next 100 years, though you can be sure there will be plenty of bumps along the way. If we're fortunate, we'll get through it without civil wars, nuclear meltdowns, racial unrest or new, devastating diseases.

I'm the eternal optimist. I think all those things are possible. Indeed, if we can achieve them, it won't matter if we see flying cars by the end of this century or by the end of this millennium.

Here's to the 2000s! *(Jan. 1, 2000)*

IT REMAINS IN DOUBT WHEN CITY WILL SHED EYESORE OF AMSHACK

1978.

I'm finishing up my last year of college. Jimmy Carter is approaching the middle of his presidency. Union Station is shut down. Trains are temporarily routed to a nearby trailer.

St. Louisans are promised that a new train terminal will be built.

Fast forward 23 years. My son is in his third year of college. Jimmy Carter is now as well-known for his humanitarian efforts as for his presidency.

And St. Louisans are promised that a new train terminal will be built.

That's right, boys and girls. Put on your party hats and get out your noisemakers. Wednesday marks the 23rd anniversary of Amshack!

My, how the time goes by. It seems it was only yesterday that we were celebrating Amshack's 22nd anniversary.

Dubbed "Amshack" by St. Louisans, the temporary station is located between an industrial area and a parking lot downtown. It consists of five trailers pulled together. From those trailers, at 550 South 16th Street, trains pull into and out of St. Louis each day. St. Louis, a city that was once second in rail traffic only to Chicago, now settles for this rail site.

Union Station was once the proud home of around-the-clock rail service, a beehive of activity. But as travelers moved to planes and their personal automobiles, the station was used less and less. In 1978, officials saw little need for the cavernous building with so few trains. Train service was moved to the temporary site, east of the station. Officials promised to build a new station for the trains.

In 1985, Union Station reopened with a new purpose, now the home of a major hotel, glittery shops and a myriad of restaurants. But unlike cities such as Washington, whose Union Station houses stores and restaurants but also operates an up-to-date train facility, St. Louis made no plans for trains in its Union Station, and the "temporary" station remained.

Meanwhile, the temporary station — located down a dusty, cobblestone street, past Postal Service trailers — is more reminiscent of a station in a small town in the middle of nowhere than one that serves a major metropolitan area. Newcomers who pull into St. Louis each day are greeted with an ugly welcome to the Gateway City.

It's not as if no one realizes that this problem exists.

As far back as 1987, discussions were being held about building a "multimodal transportation terminal." This was going to be a super terminal that would combine Amtrak, MetroLink, Bi-State and Greyhound stations in one spot, along with a pad to be used by helicopters.

"The design calls for a futuristic, modular-looking building to take shape at the corner of Jefferson Avenue and Scott Street, just south of Highway 40," the *Post-Dispatch* reported in 1992. "An opening date is at least two years away."

Clearly the key words there were "at least."

St. Louis mayors as far back as Jim Conway have had the issue of what to do with the trains on their plate. Last spring, then-Mayor Clarence Harmon announced that a deal had finally been struck between the city and Amtrak to build what is now being called the St. Louis Gateway Transportation Center. At that time, city officials said that the new station could be built by next year.

But doubt remains.

Barbara Geisman, Mayor Francis Slay's director of development, conceded Monday that the current station "is a big embarrassment to the city."

"We've learned that there are a number of land agreements that still need to get done to make this project work, so we're not as far along as we would like," she said. "But we've gotten the city counselor's office involved in it, and we're going to get this thing done as soon as we can."

Richard A. Eichhorst, president of the American Association of Railroaders Inc. and a proponent of a new station, is taking a wait-and-see attitude this time. "I'm from Missouri," he said. "Show me the shovel that turns the first bit of dirt for a new station, and then I'll believe it." *(Oct. 30, 2001)*

FRANK QUESTION ABOUT TASTE

Jack Randall can't understand why the city's so concerned about a hot dog.

Seriously. As Dave Barry would say, I'm not making this up.

Randall is thinking about opening a small restaurant at Seventh and Olive streets and wants to erect a giant, vertical weenie on the corner of the building.

The city's Heritage and Urban Design Commission is wary of the weenie. It's leaning toward a horizontal one rather than a vertical one.

So what's going on?

Let's start at the beginning.

Randall is a lawyer in St. Louis who owns and has renovated several buildings downtown, including the one in which he and his wife live. He also owns the Randall Gallery at 999 North 13th Street.

Randall explains the hot-dog story this way: His wife's nephew owns a 24-hour convenience store in Chicago that's part of a chain there. "The stores are very dangerous," Randall said. "They're usually robbed twice a week."

Worried about the nephew's safety, Randall has been urging him to move to St. Louis and open a small downtown restaurant. Randall owns a building at the corner of Seventh and Olive and thinks it might be a good location for such a place.

Enter the hot dog.

"I thought that a good way to attract people to the place might be the use of a three-dimensional sign element," he said.

Randall had in mind some of the signs used in California, particularly during an earlier age, where signs actually made it clear — without reading — what the buildings were.

Randall's idea was to have a large, vertical hot dog on the corner of the building. "I thought the sign would romanticize the restaurant," he said, and bring a little color to downtown. "People could use the sign as a landmark — 'Meet me under the big weenie,' for instance," he said.

Then Randall ran into the Heritage and Urban Design Commission. The encounter had a slow start.

"It had been a pretty boring meeting," Randall said.

But when he made his request, the result was a weenie debate about hot dogs.

"The commission asked me if I thought the weenie would be better lying down," Randall said. "I thought they were kidding."

They weren't, and commission members began to debate the pros and cons of weeniedom.

The commission took no position. Instead, it took the case under advisement and promised a decision at a later date. To date, Randall hasn't heard back.

"We'll see what they say," Randall said. "It's not firm that we're going to do this. We'll see what happens."

Actually, a desire to put a giant hot dog on a building is not out of character for Randall. He doesn't mind stirring things up a bit. It makes life interesting, he says.

And a weenie on a building would make downtown more interesting, he adds, suggesting that Midwestern cities often suffer from "boring" buildings. "Downtowns shouldn't have awnings on all their buildings and be made to look like malls," he said. "When it comes to tourism, the greatest gimmick in the world is having something interesting when people go there."

But St. Louisans are sometimes too conservative for interesting, he says.

Randall has had some interesting ideas for the city, but hasn't had much success in selling them.

"In many cities, signs on buildings are part of the fun," he said. "At one time, I was interested in putting lights up along Grand like the neon lights on Broadway. But I was told that it was too garish."

Officials weren't too high on another of his ideas either. Randall had suggested "taking the Old Post Office and turning it into a big toilet."

"It would be a big place where people could change clothes, change diapers, use clean bathrooms, maybe watch TV while they rested," he said. That idea never took off either.

Randall still thinks that Lambert Field would be better served if the airport encouraged local food places, like the O.T. Hodge Chili or Ted Drewes, to open outlets there. "It would give tourists a real flavor of St. Louis," he said. "It wouldn't be the same old food that you could find in almost any airport in America."

Meanwhile, though, Randall waits for the commission to make a decision.

"I don't know if they're pro-weenie or anti-weenie," he

said. "I'll just have to sit back and wait." *(Nov. 26, 1993)*

HOW WE TURNED PEEPING TOM

So what were we last week? Voyeurs or mere news consumers who wanted to be kept up to date?

Americans scrambled to their radios and TV sets last Friday night, the minute they heard that O.J. Simpson was trying to flee justice.

Sensing the public's interest, the stations quickly switched to the slow-motion "chase," often abandoning their regular programming. KMOX radio — the voice of the baseball Cardinals — interrupted the ballgame. NBC interrupted the National Basketball Association playoffs, later showing the game and the chase simultaneously, in split-screen fashion. The situation was given the kind of coverage reserved for, say, the death of a sitting president.

We rushed to our sets and stayed glued, especially after hearing that Simpson had a gun and was threatening to kill himself. Like moviegoers, we watched the footage from helicopters as Simpson traveled from Orange County, California to his home in the Brentwood section of Los Angeles.

For those who live in LA, there was a special treat. They could — and did — line the freeways and watch as this drama unfolded before them. Countless Angelenos took to the sides of freeways to watch the former rent-a-car spokesman or cheer him on.

What is it that makes so many of us eager to see tragedy? Why do some of us get adrenaline rushes at such occasions?

Some of it, I suppose, can be attributed to human nature. Indeed, some of the same people who are shaking their heads now and feeling superior to those who lined those LA freeways are the ones who cause traffic tie-ups whenever there's a major car accident on the other side of the highway by rubbernecking to see every gruesome detail.

More than 13 years ago, I was sent to Kansas City to cover the Hyatt Regency tragedy, in which the skywalks of that hotel collapsed at a Friday night tea dance, killing 114 people and injuring 200.

I got to Kansas City in the middle of the night, and what shocked me, perhaps even as much as the deaths and injuries, was the gawkers. Hundreds of them lined Kansas City's McGee Street to watch the dead and the injured being taken out of the hotel's lobby. Some of them brought binoculars; others brought cameras.

When I asked one woman why she had come, she told me: "This is exciting. It's tragic, too, but it's the kind of thing I'll probably never see again in my whole life. I just wanted to see."

The same was the case with Simpson. Many of those watching the tragedy "just wanted to see."

You could almost hear an announcer: "Will O.J. kill himself? Will the police shoot at him? Or will he somehow get away from the officers now hot in pursuit? Tune in tomorrow, same Bat Time, same Bat Channel . . . ."

Try as we might to excuse ourselves from our shameless viewing of the unraveling of Simpson, most of us were voyeurs. We wanted every tidbit of Simpson information, and the news media provided.

Those who were later critical of the media and of the public who watched the Simpson saga reminded me of people who say that they never watch television; or if they do, only PBS.

I suspect that even the most highbrow and intellectual among us were riveted to the set last Friday night.

Simpson's the hot topic right now. He made the covers of Time and Newsweek this week; his was the lead story for several days in newspapers across the country; his football cards — and even those of his best friend, former teammate Al Cowlings — began to command top prices.

Three paperback books about Simpson are expected to reach stores within two weeks. And, just as one can sense when a storm is coming on, I feel a made-for-TV movie coming on.

Like it or not, we're human, and we're fascinated by everything about Simpson these days. In my own newsroom this week, whenever Simpson appeared in the courtroom, my colleagues and I gathered around the set to watch. Then we'd comment: "He looks so thin," "Did you see those circles around his eyes?" "I wonder if he's on a food strike?"

And we're newspeople, folks who aren't usually moved by this sort of thing.

No, when it comes to O.J. Simpson, most Americans have gone beyond being mere consumers of the news to becoming electronic Peeping Toms.

And we just can't help ourselves. *(June 24, 1994)*

CHECK BACK WITH ME JAN. 1 ON THIS Y2K COMPUTER THING

It was only a movie.

Well, I'm either the biggest fool who roamed the Earth in the 20th century or one of the smartest fellows of the 1900s.

And only time will tell.

That became abundantly clear Sunday night as NBC aired "Y2K," a made-for-TV movie about the world in chaos on New Year's Eve 1999. In the film, an F-18 Navy jet in the Marshall Islands crashes at 12:01 a.m. in the first place to see the millennium change. Major disasters soon follow throughout the world, including power outages in Times Square, malfunctioning medical equipment and threats of nuclear breakdown.

NBC and some affiliates were so concerned about this movie — and what Americans might think — that they issued an on-air disclaimer:

"This program is a purely fictional thriller. The characters and situations are not based on fact. This program does not suggest or imply that any of these events could actually occur."

Like some rube is sitting on his sofa watching TV and saying, "See, Gertrude, that's why I don't trust them there computers."

It's not 1938, folks, and this isn't Orson Welles' "War of the Worlds." I like to think that most folks are a little more sophisticated and know the difference between a movie and real life.

If I sound a bit skeptical, it's because I am. The Y2K computer bug is a result of programming shortcuts that used two digits to denote the year. Experts have warned that systems could fail if computers are not fixed to properly read 2000.

I understand the computer bug. But I also think we've all gotten enough warning to do something about it. Computer whizzes at the newspaper, for instance, have spent all year going through all of our computers to make them Y2K compliant. My computer at home was purchased after the date that the glitch was supposedly fixed.

I'm not being naive about this. I realize that Y2K may have an effect on computer systems in some other countries. There is a very real possibility that some of those countries will not have had the resources to make the necessary changes there. But I feel fairly confident that the computers in this country will be in good shape. I don't think most of us will be living in bomb shelters on New Year's Day, eating canned rations and freeze-dried food.

It seems as if every other day in the mail I'm receiving something from my bank or insurance company or other agency that I deal with assuring me that my items are Y2K-safe. I know that they've worked on this and tested things out, and I have no real reason not to believe them.

Some would accuse me of having a false sense of security. I don't know about all of that. We'll have some extra groceries around the house around New Year's. But it won't be because of Y2K. It will be because it will be during the holidays, and we always have extra groceries in during that time, not to mention the leftovers. Plus, our son will be home from college, bringing his healthy appetite with him, and we'll keep the fridge well-stocked.

But don't look for me among those rushing to the bank to take my money out. I've never been one to think that old money-under-the-mattress thing was a good idea, and I have enough confidence in my bank that I'm not expecting my funds to disappear, for reasons other than normal ones, like Christmas shopping.

So all of this makes me either wise and level-headed, or an insane idiot. And none of us will really know until Jan. 1, 2000.

At that time, you'll be able to come up to me, shake my hand and congratulate me on being a wise man.

Either that, or you'll be able to tap me on the shoulder, look me in the eye, and tell me what a fool I was.

Needless to say, I'm counting on the former. *(Nov. 23, 1999)*

OUR JUNK MAIL HAS BECOME DIGITAL; ISN'T TECHNOLOGY WONDERFUL?

There was a time, maybe 15 years ago or so, when the arrival of a fax meant something important.

In this newsroom, faxes got special attention. They meant "urgent," that something was breaking, some piece of news too immediate to simply mail.

Over time, however, that started to change. Faxes arrived with get-rich-quick schemes, announcement of fast-food restaurant openings, and press releases about things no one cared about. No surprise, then, that faxes these days get considerably less attention than they once did.

Now e-mail seems to be the rage, and I'm beginning to resent the person who invented it. I don't mind e-mail letters. I get maybe 300 e-mail letters a week, and I'm happy to get them and respond to them.

What bothers me is the fact that every cockamamie idea, every "make money in your own home" scheme, every conspiracy theory about black helicopters flying overhead seems to arrive in my e-mailbox. Now that we've learned to mass mail e-mail, we've come up with the Internet equivalent of the annoying sales call during the dinner hour.

So while I once waited in anticipation for e-mail, wondering what new and wonderful idea was being sent my way, now I sometimes grimace when I receive a great deal of it. It's become a blessing and a curse.

Don't believe me? Come, take a look at some of the e-mail I've received in the last week alone.

Let's see: Barnes & Noble has written to me to tell me that they can find any book for me that's out of print. While I appreciate that unsolicited information, I don't think my life would have been worse had I not known it.

Someone has sent me e-mail asking me not to buy gas from Exxon or Mobil, the theory being that they are the two largest oil companies and if we stopped buying they'd lower their prices and others would follow suit. Somehow I doubt it, especially since the two are now one company.

I've received an ad from a mortgage company that reads: "Mortgage companies make you wait. They demand to interview you. They intimidate you. And all of that is while they decide if they even want to do business with you." But if I just "click here," this company will be able to help me. Uh-huh.

Oh, here's something. A company wants to tell me all about the "hot new products for summer." They range from "all the essential equipment for your next trip to the beach or your backyard barbecue." Living in St. Louis, the closest beach to me is probably Times Beach, and I don't think I'll be surfing anywhere near there.

Here's an e-mail with the words "$200 in free gas." That is, if I join a certain travel club. If I do, my name will go into a lottery where I might win $200 in free gas. But you can't win if you don't enter, so I'll have to go gasless.

And if you've been watching your snail-mail box hoping for that letter from Publishers Clearing House, here's something even better. With the words "imminent winner" in the message field, I have this: "It's coming soon: the day the Publishers Clearing House Prize Patrol could visit the Freeman home to award a $1,000,000 prize! I urge you to complete and submit the attached $1,000,000 PRIZE AWARD ENTRY REGISTRATION to enter today! If you respond to this notice right away and are selected the winner, the Prize Patrol will knock on your door to award Gregory Freeman a $1,000,000 SuperPrize!" And that personal e-mail, ladies and gentlemen, came directly from Jennifer Mallory, the prize coordinator.

I've received all of these in the past week, despite the fact that I have a program that's supposed to filter out the junk mail. So let me make one small request: If you were planning to send me any e-mail selling me anything, offering a get-rich-quick scheme or offering me something free that really isn't, do me a big favor.

Don't send it to me. *(April 24, 2001)*

'BIG-BONEDED' COLUMNIST TACKLES WEIGHTY MATTERS

I'm a big man.

Oh, I don't mean big in importance or anything like that. In the pecking order of things, I'm probably somewhere near the bottom of the food chain.

But in size, I'm what someone once called "big-boneded."

I don't know how big my bones actually are. But there's quite a bit of meat to go around those bones. Enough meat to fill a meat locker if I were a cow.

I've always been a big guy. It's just that I'm bigger these days than I was in high school.

I find that people are all over the spectrum on the issue of weight. Some think those who are overweight are examples of people who have no self-control. They imagine these people to be folks who have no discipline, who can't even pull their lives together.

Others think that overweight people are the most in control of all. They argue that people who are overweight are those with complete self-confidence, who don't believe that the only way to have friends, or succeed in life, or be happy or whatever is to starve yourself to death.

Despite what everyone says, I want to lose weight. Not because I fear I have no self-control. I'm very much in control. Not because I'm trying to get more friends or become more successful or anything like that. I just wouldn't mind being thinner.

It's not like I haven't tried.

I've tried several diets over the years. Twice, I've gone on liquid protein diets. With those, you don't eat anything for a time. Instead, you drink special shakes, made with enough protein and vitamins to sustain a person for a while.

Those were great. I lost nearly 100 pounds. While I wasn't svelte — I've never been skinny — I was pretty pleased with the weight I'd lost.

Then came the hard part. Keeping it off.

You don't stay on liquid protein diets forever. Eventually you've got to eat. That was my downfall.

You see, I like food. Good food. Rich food. Fattening food.

Of course, every time I turn around, I find that the things I love are bad for me. Mexican food, one of my passions, is bad for you, they say. Movie popcorn is bad for you. Chinese food is bad for you. And all of those, they say, can be unbelievably fattening.

But they taste so good.

Despite it all, I'm not giving up on my weight-loss hopes.

Part of that has to do with my wife.

Last year, she joined Weight Watchers. She lost a lot of weight, and she's kept it off. So she suggested I join.

I wasn't so sure about it at first. My thoughts ran to a heavyset aunt who was on the program 25 years ago. I remembered her drinking a cup of coffee with liquid saccharine — that clear stuff that was so sweet it was bitter if you put a drop on your tongue — and following that with huge hunks of chocolate cake. I don't know if she ever lost any weight.

But seeing my wife slim down before my very eyes made an impression on me.

So a few weeks ago, I joined. Every Saturday, we go in and get weighed. Then we listen to a group leader who talks to us about strategies for eating better and paying closer attention to what we eat. He talks to us about how we can be smarter about eating. To see this guy, you'd never think he was ever overweight. He says he used to be heavy years ago but has learned how to take weight off and keep it off.

Since joining, I've been trying to watch what I eat. I've been eating things like rice and pasta — which are actually low in calories — and laying off the sauces. I've been limiting my visits to fast-food places and eating more Japanese food like sushi, which I've always enjoyed and which is generally low in fat. I've been laying off big breakfasts like waffles with sausage and eggs, and turning to smaller ones like oatmeal and an English muffin.

So far it's been working. I've lost 5 1/2 pounds. Not a lot in the overall scheme of things, perhaps, but a start. I've been conditioning myself to be patient with the results. I didn't gain all this weight overnight, and I'm not going to lose it overnight either. But if I can lose it slowly and methodically, I think the chances are better that I'll keep it off.

At least that's what I'm hoping.

So it's off to eating better and more exercise for me. More sliced cucumbers with lemon juice as snacks and fewer powdered doughnuts. *(March 17, 1995)*

SENSIBLE SHOES CAN CHANGE A PERSON'S OUTLOOK ON LIFE

Comfort over fashion.

I write today in praise of comfortable shoes.

It may seem like a topic of little importance, particularly in comparison to some of the major issues facing the world. Yet shoes can make a difference between whether a person is easygoing or ill-mannered.

I was inspired to write this column after purchasing a pair of shoes from a local shoe store last weekend. My old pair of tennis shoes were worn, dirty, a bit uncomfortable and had seen their better days. I decided to pop in and buy a new pair. What I found was a pair of walking shoes. The salesman measured both my feet and brought out a pair of shoes that I fell in love with. I bought them without hesitation.

The shoes aren't much to look at. My son teased me about them, and called them "Dad shoes." But I love them. When I'm wearing them, it feels almost as if I'm walking barefoot.

Since I've bought them, I've found myself with more bounce to the ounce, with more pep in my step, with more glide in my stride. My mood has improved, and I'm feeling great.

There was a time in my life when I was a slave to fashion, as far as shoes were concerned. Back in the '70s, I had a pair of platform shoes with one-inch soles and four-inch heels. I loved them until one of my heels got caught and I fell down a flight of stairs in high school. That was the end of my high-heeled experiences.

For many years, I wore only leather dress shoes for work, without variation. It didn't matter if they weren't that comfortable; it was what you wore to work.

But something's changed in recent years. Maybe it's wisdom that's come with middle age. I've traded in my old master of fashion and picked up a new master: comfort.

I no longer care much about fashion when it comes to shoes. I want them to be comfortable. If the shoes are comfortable, that's all I need.

There's little in the world that's better than a comfortable pair of shoes. *(July 1, 1999)*

RAMS' NEWEST FAN THINKS TEAM'S HARD WORK WILL PAY OFF — NO TRASH REQUIRED

Regular readers know that I'm not much of a sports fan. One friend calls me "sports impaired."

I never played sports in school (other than a half-semester on the tennis team in high school). I've never been one to spend my Saturdays and Sundays glued to the set watching the various games that are shown one after the other.

That's a complete contrast to my brother-in-law, who I consider to be "Mr. Sports." Not only does he play just about every sport, he loves to watch them all on television as well. I often joke that he probably even finds golf matches exciting. (Yes, I know, someone really does get a thrill out of watching them.) Even my wife likes to watch figure skating competitions.

Being sports impaired, I'm already grumbling that we're going to have to get through the Winter Olympics before we get any regular programming back on television. We'll have to get the life story of every athlete who competes: "When John Doe was twelve, he tore a cuticle, and doctors told him he'd never be able to compete in snowboarding again. But young John was determined. Every day he exercised his hand and nursed his nail with an herbal dressing. And today, he's here in Salt Lake City, representing the United States at the 2002 Winter Olympic Games!"

So I'm not that psyched about the Winter Olympics.

But I am psyched about the Rams.

On Sunday afternoon, you'll find me parked in front of our television set, cheering the Rams on.

I've been doing this now for the past couple of months. It started when I was recuperating from surgery. I couldn't walk, so I watched an inordinate amount of television, including Rams games. I must admit I got into them and found myself rooting for the team.

"Let's go, Kurt Warner," I'd yell from my bed. "Way to go, Marshall Faulk!"

I got to know who the players were, even got to know

some of their records.

When other teams started trash-talking the Rams, I took offense. But I was happy that we didn't lower ourselves to that standard. The Rams took their opponents seriously, concentrating on the next game.

That brings us to Philadelphia. Such trash-talking I've never seen, not just from the team but from the Philly news media. And not only are they trashing our team, they're trashing our town.

That's OK. Once again, our Rams aren't lowering themselves to the level of those in Philadelphia. No trash-talking on our part. We're Midwesterners, after all. We're not loud and boisterous, like some from other parts of the country.

I think that's another reason I like the Rams. It's like Goofus and Gallant, the comic strip characters I used to read in Boys' Life magazine when I was a kid. Goofus was always doing something stupid or saying something nasty about someone. But Gallant would always handle the matter differently, always doing what he was supposed to do and winning in the end.

The Rams, you see, are Gallant. And, yes, the Philadelphia fans are Goofus. Let them trash-talk us, I say. We'll be the winners in the end.

This all reminds me of a situation 15 years ago, when I was involved with an effort to try to bring a national journalism convention to St. Louis. We were competing with New York, and most felt that there was no way the organization's board would pick St. Louis over New York. Even the New Yorkers laughed at us. New York has everything, they thought. Why would anyone select St. Louis?

Well, those of us from St. Louis worked hard. We put together a top-notch video for our presentation, with the mayor, the governor and even Ozzie Smith urging the organization to come to St. Louis. We got a top St. Louis businessman to join us when we made the pitch, to talk about why St. Louis would be a good location for a business.

And in the end, by one vote, St. Louis beat New York for that convention.

That's why, when all is said and done, I look for the Rams to head off to New Orleans and the Super Bowl where, with Mike Martz at the helm, there will be no trash-talking on our end. Only hard work and solid sportsmanship.

I may be sports impaired, but I know a good team when I see one. *(Jan. 27, 2002)*

About the Author

Gregory B. Freeman was a *Post-Dispatch* columnist, an unbashedly proud son of St. Louis and a champion for racial harmony. His death from heart failure on Dec. 31, 2002, at age 46, brought an outpouring of grief and fond memories from readers who had been following his columns for over a decade. The response was so great that the *Post-Dispatch* published a commemorative section in his honor on Jan. 5, 2003. On the same day, hundreds of St. Louisans came to his memorial service, spilling outside of Washington University's Graham Chapel and into an annex.

Greg will be remembered as both a genuinely nice person and a man of great courage. During his adulthood, he battled kidney disease, prostate cancer and muscular dystrophy. No one can remember ever hearing him complain. More often they heard expressions of gratitude, — to his sister Cheryl McKinney, for donating a kidney when he needed a transplant, to his wife, Elizabeth, his mother, Doris and son, Will, for their love, friendship and support, and to his readers for their letters and calls.

He was quite a journalist, too. A triple threat - someone called him. He had hosted KWMU-FM's "St. Louis on the Air" since 1999. And he also moderated a television show, "Mosaic with Greg Freeman" from 1997 to 2001. The show won two local Emmy awards.

Greg was born in St. Louis and grew up in the Penrose neighborhood. He graduated from Washington University with a degree in Spanish in 1978. He worked at the old Washington (D.C.) Star, the St. Louis American, the Oakland Press in Pontiac, Mich., and the Belleville News-Democrat before he joined the *Post-Dispatch* in 1980 as a reporter. Freeman covered politics and city hall, then became an assistant editor before moving on to column writing.

Greg supported many programs in the community, including several that assisted African-American journalists.

Greg Freeman: A Gentleman, A Gentle Man